P. Hoey

AN IRISH PILGRIM'S GUIDE TO ROME

Great Jubilee o

GW00362731

VERITAS

First published 1999 by
Veritas Publications
7-8 Lower Abbey Street
Dublin 1

ISBN 1 85390 515 1

British Library Cataloguing
in Publication Data.
A catalogue record for
this book is available
from the British Library.

Designed by Bill Bolger
Map drawings by Barbara Croatto
Cover Photograph: View of St Peter's Square. Reproduced by permission of *L'Osservatore Romano*, Vatican City.
Printed in the Republic of Ireland by Betaprint Ltd, Dublin

I am very much in debt to God, who gave me so much grace that through me many people were born again in God... All this was for a people newly come to belief whom the Lord took from the very ends of the earth as he promised long ago through his prophets: 'To you the nations will come from the ends of the earth....'

St Patrick (d. 461), Confession

All we Irish, inhabitants of the world's edge,
are disciples of Saints Peter and Paul.

St Columban (d. 615), 5th Letter

Since we are travellers and Pilgrims in the world,
let us ever ponder on the end of the road, that is on our life,
for the end of our roadway is our home.

St Columban, 8th Sermon

CONTENTS

SECTION I – ABOUT ROME

SECTION II– SUGGESTED ITINERARIES

SECTION III
RELIGIOUS HOUSES WITH IRISH CONNECTIONS 117

SECTION IV
A SELECTION OF PRAYERS AND HYMNS FOR THE PILGRIM

1. Na Paidreacha Coitianta
2. Hymns

SECTION V – ROME JUBILEE 2000 CALENDAR

INTRODUCTION

Ireland and Rome have had a longstanding and, at times, somewhat ambiguous relationship. Almost since the dawn of Christianity in our country, the Irish have felt drawn to the city of the Apostles and martyrs, to visit their tombs and to see their successors. Taking diverse routes, journeying by land and by sea, across the Alps and along the coast, our ancestors in the faith have come to Rome to pray, to see, to study, and above all, to be in the place where, by visiting the tombs of St Peter and St Paul, they can be close to the historical Christ, known by one and sensed intimately in the being of the other.

One early Irish pilgrim, intensely spiritual by nature, voiced his unease with what he saw in Rome when he wrote, 'Who to Rome goes, much labour, little profit knows; For God, on earth though long you've sought him, You'll miss at Rome unless you've brought him.' The ambiguity of the relationship is to be found in the fact that Ireland was never incorporated into the Roman Empire, and has always held a healthy respect for its independence. The Irish mind, therefore, while it is consistently well disposed to Rome, likes to be free, Celtic and original. The pull and the tug of the relationship continues unabated and now enters its third millennium.

Representatives of an ancient tradition, the Irish in Rome at present came together almost three years ago, to prepare a warm and efficient welcome for those who will mark the Jubilee of the year 2000 in this city. A committee known as the Irish Houses in Rome Jubilee Committee, comprising the various houses in Rome with Irish roots, together with the Ambassadors of Ireland to the Holy See and to Italy, has taken a number of initiatives to effect this. A general guide to Rome would not suit an Irish pilgrim after such a long and particular history. An Irish pilgrim's guide to Rome is needed, where aspects of this relationship can be explored and the eternal verities of Rome revisited. A central office to help pilgrims during the year has been set up in the Irish College and a calendar of ceremonies and social events prepared for the Irish in Rome, both resident and pilgrim.

The Chapel of St Columbanus, built in 1954 in the Crypt of the Basilica of St Peter, was renovated by the Committee with the financial support of the Irish Knights of St Columbanus and the bishops of Ireland. On 22 June 1999, it was dedicated by His Grace, Most Reverend Seán Brady, Archbishop of Armagh and Primate of All Ireland. Situated beside the tomb of St Peter, this Chapel represents the closeness of Ireland to the heart of Rome.

When the Jubilee 2000 has been marked and the third millennium firmly established, it is the hope of the Irish Houses in Rome Jubilee Committee that this *Irish Pilgrim's Guide to Rome* will serve as a souvenir of a historic visit to Rome and may evoke many wonderful memories.

The gratitude of the Committee goes to the author of this guide, Fr Padhraic O'Loughlin, a priest of St Columban's Missionary Society, who, together with Mrs Mary Wisley Venturini, Editor, *Wanted in Rome*, Sr Mary O'Duffy SMG, and Br John Heneghan CFC, Christian Brothers, put so much effort and expertise into preparing it.

Monsignor John Fleming
Chairperson

Fr Liam McCarthy OFM
Secretary

IRISH HOUSES IN ROME JUBILEE COMMITTEE
The following have participated in meetings of the Irish Houses in Rome Jubilee Committee:

Monsignor John Fleming, Pontifical Irish College, *Chairperson*
Father Liam McCarthy OFM, *Secretary*
H. E. Eamon O Tuathail, Ambassador of Ireland to the Holy See
H. E. Joseph Small, Ambassador of Ireland to Italy
H. E. Gearóid Ó Broin, Ambassador of Ireland to Finland (formerly, Ambassador of Ireland to the Holy See) and Mrs R. Ó Broin
Mr Michael Tierney, Secretary, Embassy of Ireland to the Holy See
Dr Giuseppe Lamponi, (formerly Secretary, Embassy to the Holy See)
Sister Amadeus IBVM
Sister Margaret McMahon LCM
Sister Bertranda Mulryan OP
Sister Mary O'Duffy SMG
Mrs Mary Wilsey Venturini, Editor, *Wanted in Rome*
Father James Bermingham SPS
Father Patrick McSweeney, OFM
Father Michael Brennock OSA
Brother Stephen Buckley SAC
Father Sean Cannon CSsR
Father Michael Dunleavy OP
Father John Fortune IC
Brother John Heneghan CFC, Christian Brothers
Father William Jenkinson CSSp
Father Padhraic O'Loughlin SSC
Father Kieran O'Reilly SMA

A NOTE FROM THE AUTHOR

With the publication of the Apostolic Letter *Tertio Millennio Adveniente*, 10 November 1994, Pope John Paul II announced that the end of the second millennium and the beginning of the third millennium of the Christian era would be marked by the solemn celebration of the Holy Year 2000, the 'Great Jubilee'. In the Bible, the Book of Leviticus tells of the institution of the 'jubilee year': 'You shall count off seven weeks of years... you shall have the trumpet sounded throughout all your land... And you shall hallow the fiftieth year and you shall proclaim liberty throughout the land to all its inhabitants' (Lev 25:8-12). The jubilee year was based on the principles of social justice inherent in the foundation of Israel: the land belonged to God, all was his gift to his people. The jubilee called for care of creation and of the earth: the land was to be rested and left untilled, property and belongings which had been sold were to be returned to their owners and debtors were to be freed from their debts.

Jesus Christ came to announce a year of grace (Lk 4:16-20). He came to announce a message of joy to the poor and 'to proclaim the year of the Lord's favour... to bring good news to the oppressed, to bind up the brokenhearted, to proclaim liberty to the captives and release to the prisoners' (Is 61:1-2). In Jesus Christ the history of our salvation finds its ultimate meaning. In him we have all received 'grace upon grace' (Jn 1:16).

In proclaiming the Jubilee Year 2000, the Pope continues a biblical tradition and the papal practice since 1300 of setting aside one year every twenty-five years as a Holy Year. The Great Jubilee Year 2000 has a special significance as we celebrate two thousand years of Christianity and the beginning of the third millennium. The Pope's ardent wish is that it be a time of reconciliation with God and neighbour, a year of prayer and penance, renewal and reparation, love and service of those in need.

The primary aim of this guidebook is to help Irish pilgrims coming to Rome during the Jubilee Year 2000. It seeks to combine in a simple way some basic information with some practical advice. It is hoped that the Jubilee celebration will lead pilgrims to experience something of the faith of Saints Peter and Paul, in order to confirm their own faith in Christ. It is also hoped that they will experience the sense of awe and history which is Rome, the city the Emperor Hadrian called *'Roma Aeterna'*, Eternal Rome.

This *Irish Pilgrim's Guide to Rome* draws on many well-known sources and books. For pilgrims seeking more detailed guides, the following are recommended:

Richards, Hubert, *Pilgrim to Rome: A Practical Guide* (McCrimmons 1994). An excellent guide for the Catholic pilgrim.
Blue Guide: Rome and Environs (A&C Black 1994). A detailed guide to classical and Christian Rome.
Masson, Georgina, *Companion Guide to Rome* (Companion Guides: revised by Tim Jepson, 1998). A classic.
Silke, John J., *Relics, Refugees and Rome, Being a sort of Irish Guide-Book to the Eternal City* (Rome 1975). An interesting historical survey of Ireland's connections with Rome.
Wanted in Rome. An informative magazine in English which is published every fortnight with detailed and exact up-to-date information about museums, galleries, concerts, etc. Available at all news-stands.

You will find all the information you need to know about the Jubilee events in Rome at the web site of the Jubilee Central Committee: www.jubil2000.org

THE IRISH PILGRIM

St Patrick, after his return to Ireland in 432, spent the remainder of his life walking the length and breadth of the country preaching the Gospel. The Book of Armagh contains a saying of St Patrick in which he urged the people of Ireland to be both Christians and Romans, *ut christiani ita et romani sitis*. Ancient traditions and customs indicate that going on pilgrimage was part of the Irish Christian mentality and spirituality. The lives of many Irish saints, for example, Sts Brigid, Killian, Fintan, Colmcille, Columban, invariably refer to them as 'being on pilgrimage for the love of God,' or doing so 'in the name of Christ.' St Gall (d. ca. 615), in writing about Columban and the large numbers who followed him to the continent of Europe, writes, 'Of late so many Irish are pilgrims that it would appear that the habit of travelling is part of their nature. St Molua (d. ca. 608), is quoted as saying as he set out on pilgrimage, 'Unless I see Rome, I will die soon.'

To this day there are pilgrimages to many places in Ireland where, according to either written sources or constant oral tradition, Patrick visited, preached and prayed. Well-known places are Downpatrick, the site of the Saint's tomb; Lough Derg which is known as 'Patrick's Purgatory', and Croagh Patrick where he spent an entire Lent in prayer and fasting. Many local churches and communities have annual pilgrimages to honour Our Lady, or a particular saint or holy place. Each year, Knock, where tradition says the Blessed Mother appeared to local people in the last century, continues to attract increasing numbers of pilgrims from Ireland and from abroad. Pope John Paul II visited Knock in September 1979, and spoke at the shrine:

Here I am at the goal of my journey to Ireland: the Shrine of Our Lady of Knock... I have felt a strong desire to come here, the desire to make yet another pilgrimage to the Shrine of the Mother of Christ, the Mother of the Church, the Queen of Peace... I am here then as a pilgrim, a sign of the pilgrim Church throughout the world, participating, through my presence as Peter's successor, in a very special way in the centenary celebration of this shrine.

The Catholics of Ireland have always had a very strong devotion to the successor of St Peter, the Bishop of Rome. Thus, Rome has always been a place of pilgrimage for the Irish pilgrim, a journey to profess one's faith at the tomb of the Apostle Peter who was chosen by Christ to be his Vicar on earth. The Irish pilgrim on pilgrimage to Rome for the Great Jubilee 2000 is yet another link in a long chain of tradition.

IRISH PILGRIM'S OFFICE: PONTIFICAL IRISH COLLEGE

Coláiste na nGaedheal, Via dei SS. Quattro, 1
Metro A, Station Manzoni, Metro B, Station Colosseo; Buses 81, 85, 87, 117, and 714 all pass through Piazza S. Giovanni in Laterano.

The Office for Irish Pilgrims, set up for the Jubilee Year 2000, is situated on the grounds of the Irish Pontifical College. The office will be staffed during normal office hours and will provide information regarding Jubilee events and celebrations, as well as general information. **The Pilgrims' Office will not provide a service for room or travel reservations or confirmations**. The college is always happy to welcome visitors. As you enter the college grounds, you are asked to follow the signs which lead to the **Pilgrims' Office**. There you will be given some information on the college and made welcome with a cup of tea. You will then be directed to the College Chapel, the Reception Room and the monument to Daniel O'Connell (see p. 130).

Hours of Opening:	Monday to Saturday 09.00-18.00
	Sunday 09.00-13.00
Tel. No:	0039-06-7726-3302
Fax. No:	0039-06-7726-3303
E-mail:	pilgrims@irishcollege.org

Weekly celebration of the Sacraments of Reconciliation and the Eucharist for Irish pilgrims during Jubilee Year 2000

On each Tuesday during the Jubilee Year there will be a special celebration of the Eucharist for Irish Pilgrims in the Pope's Basilica of St John Lateran at 17.00 hours. Prior to the celebration of the Mass there will be an opportunity to receive the Sacrament of Reconciliation during a Penitential Rite. For details of the Basilica see p. 83.

Group Masses

The secretary at the Pilgrims' Office will be glad to inform groups who wish to have a special Mass in one of the Irish churches of the days and times when this is possible.

Masses in English

The following is a list of churches in Rome where, at the indicated hours, there is a regular celebration of the Eucharist in English:

S. Isidoro, Via degli Artisti, 41 (Irish Franciscan Church)	Sunday 10.00 (Except during July - September)
S. Patrizio, Via Boncompagni, 31 (Irish Augustinian Church)	Sunday 10.00
Pontifical Irish College, Via dei SS. Quattro, 1	Sunday 09.30
S. Silvestro, Mass: Piazza S. Silvestro (Pallottine Fathers)	Sunday 10.00 and 17.30
S. Susanna, Via XX Settembre, 14 (American Church)	Weekdays 18.00 Saturday 18.00 Sunday 09.00 and 10.30
S. Alfonso, Via Merulana, 31 (Redemptorist Church)	Sunday 16.00

PLACES AND PEOPLE OF SPECIAL INTEREST FOR THE IRISH PILGRIM

CHURCH OF S. STEFANO ROTONDO, Via di S. Stefano
Tomb of Donnach, son of Brian Boru. (see p. 90)

CHURCH OF S. PIETRO IN MONTORIO, Via Garibaldi, Gianicolo
Tombs of O'Neill and O'Donnell. (see p. 120)

PONTIFICAL IRISH COLLEGE, Via dei SS. Quattro, 1
Daniel O'Connell Monument (see p. 129)

ST ISIDORE'S OFM, Via degli Artisti, 41
Tomb of Luke Wadding OFM (see p. 128)

IRISH CHAPEL DEDICATED TO ST COLUMBAN,
The Crypt (The Grottoes), St Peter's Basilica (see p. 72)

PALAZZO DI PROPAGANDA FIDE, Piazza di Spagna
St Oliver Plunkett was a Professor in the original College of Propaganda

ST PATRICK'S CHURCH, Via Boncompagni, 31
Shrine in honour of St Oliver Plunkett (see p. 134)

S. CLEMENTE CHURCH AND EXCAVATIONS (see p. 133)

S. GIOCCHINO – St Joachim, Piazza dei Queriti, 17
The Irish Chapel, third on the left. The Chapel, dedicated to St Patrick, has paintings of Sts Patrick, Brigid, Benignus, Brendan, Declan, Oliver Plunkett, and the prayer of St Columbanus.

Section I

About Rome

New in Rome – Useful Information

Today, the population of Rome is just under three million people. In area, the city is relatively small but it is densely populated, with the majority of people living in apartments. The historic centre where most of the important sights are located is just over 2 kms in width. Sightseeing in this area is best done on foot, so strong and comfortable shoes are recommended: many streets in Rome have some cobblestones.

Rome is a tourist attraction during the entire year, and much more so during a Holy Year. The city can be very crowded at Easter, Christmas, and during the warm and humid summer months. Spring and autumn are the ideal times for a visit, when the weather is usually pleasant and the evenings are cool. This can also be the case during the summer, so a cardigan or pullover should be packed. Warmer clothes are needed for the winter. A compact umbrella is handy at all times. It should be noted that one is not allowed to enter the Basilica of St Peter, the Vatican, the Gardens, the Museum, or any other Roman basilica or church, wearing shorts, miniskirts, or with bare shoulders.

It is advisable to carry your name, and the address and telephone number of where you are staying, in case of emergencies.

At the time of going to print the Irish Punt is worth 2.459 LIRE or .787564 EUROS.

Arrival in Rome

By train
Arrival by continental train generally means arriving at the main Rome Railway Station, *'Termini'*.

By major airline
Regular air flights usually arrive at **Fiumicino airport**, 'Leonardo da Vinci International Airport', which is approximately 35 kms from the city centre. If using public transport, on entering the arrivals hall at Fiumicino follow the signs for 'Railway Station'. A non-stop train runs from the international airport at Fiumicino to Rome Termini railway station: look for the 'Termini' platform. It leaves every hour between 07.38 and 22.08, usually at 7 minutes past the hour. The fare is ITL 15.000 and tickets can be purchased at vending machines and at the ticket office or newsagent on the right side of the Airport Railway Station.

There is another train service from the international airport which uses the ordinary commuter train system. Trains depart from the airport every 20 minutes from 06.28 to 00.28 hours: after 21.15 the last stop is *Tiburtina*. The fare depends on the distance travelled. This train does not pass through the Termini station. The taxi fare would be approximately ITL 80.000. For taxi service, see below.

There is a night bus service to Station *Tiburtina* which runs from 01.15 to 05.00 hours, and tickets for this service are bought on the bus.

By charter flight

Charter flights normally arrive at **Ciampino airport**, 'Airport GB Pastine', which is 15 kms from Rome. There is a bus service to Ciampino railway station which takes 15 minute and trains leave for Rome Termini railway station every 10-15 minutes. Tickets (ITL 2.000) are available at the news agencies in the arrival and departure halls. There is also a bus service (ITL 2.000) for the metro (Station *Anagnina*), the 'underground' rail service, with connections to all metro stops in Rome. For taxi service, see below. A taxi ride to the centre of Rome takes about 40 minutes, depending on traffic. The fare is approximately ITL 50.000.

Handicapped Visitors

The Consorzio Cooperative Integrate (CO.IN), Via Enrico Giglioli 54/a (Tel. 06-2326-75054/5), (Mon–Fri 09.00-17.00) provides information concerning the accessibility of museums, etc. for handicapped people, as well as information, in many languages, regarding guided tours, transportation, tourist packages, etc.

Taxis

Official taxis are white or yellow with a sign on top. The ordinary cab will take up to four passengers. It is not advisable to engage non-licensed taxis at the airports or railway stations. Taxis are available in special taxi ranks or may be contacted by telephone. For radio taxis ring: 06-3570; 06-3875; 06-4994; 06-6645; 06-88177. In the city there is a surcharge of ITL 5.000 for trips at night time (22.00-07.00). On Sundays and holidays there is a surcharge of ITL 2.000. There is also a surcharge for large luggage bags and for trips beyond the city boundaries. At the start of a trip, the meter will display the sum of ITL 4.500. In case of difficulties consult the multilingual card which is found in most taxis. A tip is always appreciated (appr. 10% of fare).

A taxi from Fiumicino airport to Rome costs the amount shown on the meter plus a supplement (surcharge) of ITL 11.500. A taxi ride to the centre of Rome takes about 40 minutes, depending on traffic. A taxi ride from Ciampino airport takes about 40 minutes. The fare is approximately ITL 50.000. There is a limousine service, CON.CO.R.A, available at both airports, which takes more than four passengers, with fixed fares, depending on destination.

PUBLIC TRANSPORT

The public transport system – trains, buses, trams and metro (underground train) – is generally reliable, although it can be crowded at peak hours, and prices are reasonable. Tickets are available from newspaper stands, tobacconists and in vending machines. Tickets must be bought *before* boarding. Buses and trams are boarded through the front door (if carrying a weekly or monthly ticket), otherwise through the rear door: the centre door is the exit. Single tickets, valid for journeys within 75 minutes of stamping, must be validated in the orange machine near the rear door. Single train and metro tickets must be validated in the platform stamping machines. Weekly and monthly tickets need not be validated but should be completed with name and date of birth and must be produced when officially requested. There are plans for new electronic bus passes.

METRO

Metro trains run from 05.30 until 23.30. An entrance to the metro is marked with a large sign bearing a white **M** on a red background. There are two metro lines that intersect at Termini railway station:

Line A connects an area near the Vatican (Station Ottaviano-San Pietro and Station Cipro-Musei Vaticani) with the south-east of the city (Station Anagnina), near Ciampino airport.

Line B connects the north-east of the city (Station Rebibbia) with the south of the city (Station Laurentina), just beyond the EUR metro stop.

BUSES

Buses generally run from 05.30 until midnight (consult signs at bus stops for exceptions). A single Metrebus ticket costs ITL 1.500 and, after stamping, is valid for more than one bus or tram journey, provided journeys are made within 75 minutes. A day pass, valid for multiple trips on all transport systems, costs ITL 6.000, a weekly travel pass costs ITL 24.000, and a monthly travel pass costs ITL 50.000. The weekly ticket can be purchased in ticket vending machines and in the tobacconists at the Termini Station (they are not available in other tobacconists).

Monthly tickets are available in all tobacconists at the beginning of each month.

DOCUMENTS/CREDIT CARDS

Irish citizens need a valid passport which should be kept under lock and key, along with other valuable documents. If staying overnight in a hotel or guest-house (pensione), it is necessary to produce a passport. Keeping a photocopy of important documents in a separate place can be helpful.

When property is lost or stolen in Rome one should go immediately to a police station (*Carabinieri, Comissariato, Questura*) to report the loss and to receive a copy of the official report, which is required when claiming insurance and replacing lost airline tickets, passports and travellers' cheques. If credit cards or travellers' cheques are lost or stolen, their loss should be reported immediately to the firm that issued them. As in all tourist cities, there can be problems with pickpockets and bag-snatchers, especially in places frequented by tourists. You should carry only the money and documents you need, in a safe inside pocket.

Each of the major credit card companies provides a 24-hour emergency telephone service for lost or stolen credit cards: *American Express* (Tel: 800-72282); *Eurocard, Mastercard, Visa* (Tel: 800-167-018548); Diners (Tel: 800-167-864064). An emergency service specifically for International Visitors is provided by *Master Card* (Tel. toll free 800-167-870866) and *Visa* (Tel: toll free 800-167-877232).

EMBASSIES

Embassy of Ireland to the Holy See,
Via Giacomo Medici 1, Roma 00153,
Tel. 06-581-0777; Fax 06-589-5709 (see p. 120)

Embassy of Ireland to Italy,
Piazza di Campitelli 3, 00186 Roma.
Tel: 06-697-9121; Fax: 06-679-2354/697-91231.
All queries in relation to passports and consular matters should be directed to the Embassy of Ireland to Italy. Office Hours: 10.00-12.30; 15.00-16.30 (see p. 59)

MONEY – BANKS – CURRENCY EXCHANGE MACHINES – ATMS

The monetary unit is the Italian lira (ITL) and the Euro. The lira exchange rate can fluctuate quite a bit with non-Euro currencies. The most secure way to carry money is to use travellers' cheques, Eurocheques, Smart Cards or credit cards. The commission can be high when cashing cheques.

Banks are open Monday-Friday from 08.00-13.30; and again in the afternoon 14.30-16.00. Some banks open on Saturday mornings in the centre and business areas, from 09.00-13.00. There are currency exchange machines in operation at all times at some banks in the centre of the city, and currency exchange shops (Cambio) open during business hours. Telegraphic money orders can be received or sent at all post offices: a transfer takes 1-3 days. A number of banks have ATM facilities:

- with *Eurocard, Master Card* and *Visa*, use services offered by the Istituto Bancario San Paolo di Torino, Credito Italiano and Banca di Roma;
- with *Eurocard* use the facilities of Banca Commerciale Italiana;
- with *Visa* use the facilities provided by Banca Nazionale del Lavoro.

TELEPHONES

The sign indicating a telephone is a circular one displaying the emblem of a telephone receiver. Most telephones now work with phone cards, which are available in most bars, newspaper kiosks and tobacconists. It is necessary to tear off the corner of the card along the perforated line. For international enquiries, ring 176. Reduced rates apply from 22.00 - 08.00 hours, Mon-Sat and all day on Sundays and holidays. The international code for the Republic of Ireland is 00353; for the North of Ireland dial 0044. There are centres for international telephone calls in many areas, such as the main railway station, Termini, and the main post office, at Piazza San Silvestro, 19, which is open on weekdays 09.00-18.00; Saturdays 09.00-14.00; Sundays 09.00-18.00.

CAFES AND BARS

It is more expensive to eat sitting down than standing up, and it is much more expensive to eat sitting outside. If taking refreshments standing, read the list of items, which is available beside the cashier's desk, pay the cashier, and bring the receipt to the person at the bar. If sitting at a table inside or outside the cafe/bar, there is waiter service and the bill is paid on leaving.

PUBLIC TOILETS

Apart from public toilets in the centre of Rome, the Vatican area, and museums and galleries, there are few public toilets. Bars and restaurants are required to provide facilities to customers. In the Vatican there are public toilets near the centre of the colonnade on the right of St Peter's Square, also near the Arch of the Bells at the top left hand corner of the Square, and in the Museum. More public toilets will be provided during Jubilee 2000.

PHARMACIES

Pharmacies are indicated by a green or red illuminated sign in the form of a cross and are open for business during the following hours: 08.30-13.00 and 16.30-19.30. Many close on Saturday afternoons. A list on the door of a pharmacy indicates the nearest all-night pharmacy and the week-end openings hours. Visitors who are taking prescribed medicine should bring an adequate supply.

HEALTH AND HOSPITALS

Visitors are advised to have health insurance and to bring Form E111 for Euronationals when travelling. Free treatment and attention are available at the 24 hour emergency departments (Pronto Soccorso) of all major hospitals. Here is a short list of hospitals in the centre of Rome:

S. Spirito	Lungotevere Sassia, 1 (near St Peter's Square). Tel. 06-650901
S. Giovanni	Via Amba Aradam, 8 (near St John Lateran). Tel. 06-77051
S. Camillo	Cir. Gianicolense, 87 Tel. 06-58701
S. Filippo Neri	Piazza S. Maria della Pietà, 5 Tel. 06-33061
Fatebenefratelli	Piazza Fatebenefratelli, 2 Tel. 06-68371
Policlinico Gemelli	Largo A. Gemelli Tel. 06-30151

POSTAL SERVICE

Stamps (francobolli) for the Italian postal service are available in post offices and also in tobacconists displaying a sign with a white T on a dark background. Letters and postcards to EU countries cost ITL 800. Mail addressed to visiting pilgrims can be collected at the central post office, Piazza S. Silvestro 19, at window 72.

Stamps for the Vatican mail service are available in the post offices on the right and left sides of St. Peter's Square and in the Vatican Museum. The charge for postcards and letters for Europe is ITL 900.

PAPAL 'ANGELUS' AND PAPAL AUDIENCES

On Sundays and major Feastdays the Pope usually appears at a window of his residence in the Vatican to impart his blessing after reciting the Angelus. During the Jubilee Year he will appear regularly to give his blessing. He will also hold audiences in St Peter's Square or in the Pope Paul VI Hall which is located to the left of the basilica. Tickets for a papal audience can be obtained by writing to the Prefetto della Casa Pontificia, Città del Vaticano, 00120 Rome, or by going in person to the *Portone di Bronzo* (The Bronze Door) at the end of the right colonnade or by faxing 06-698 85863. Tickets are available 24 hours before the event and can be delivered to your hotel or guest house by special request or collected from the Portone di Bronzo in St Peter's Square.

RADIO JUBILEE

During the Holy Year 2000, Radio Jubilee, in conjunction with Vatican Radio, will provide a 24-hour service, with 12 hours of live broadcasting each day. The Radio Jubilaeum, as it is called, will transmit the Vatican Radio news, music, liturgical celebrations, interviews and up-to-date information. The English transmission will share the channel with Italian and French broadcasts. The channel will be broadcast on **FM 105** and **MW 527**.

PILGRIM'S CARD

There are four different cards for lone foreign pilgrims (Smart Cards).
1. The card that costs ITL 65.000 lasts for three days. It must be booked more than 15 days in advance and has to be paid by credit card. It entitles you to book papal events – other than Papal Audiences – some medical treatment, some public transport and ITL 20.000 worth of telephone calls. This card can be booked through the Vatican's **Servizio di Accoglienza Centrale per il Giubileo (SAC), Piazza S. Marcello 4a, 00186 Roma. Tel 06-696221; E-mail: sac@jubil2000.org; Website: http://www.sac.jubil2000.org**.

2. The card that costs ITL 55.000 also lasts for three days and gives you the same services as the ITL 65.000. It does not have to be booked in advance and you can buy it on arrival in Rome.

3. The card that costs ITL 13.000 is a one-day card and it entitles you to entry to the papal event of the day, provided there is still room.

4. There is a ITL 13.000 'One Day' card which provides booking for the day's events, medical services and public transport, but no telephone calls.

There are other arrangements for groups with an independent tour operator.

Tiber Boat Trips
There are plans to have regular boat trips on the Tiber.

Hours of Admission and Entrance Fees

The following is an attempt to give the opening hours and admission fees, where applicable, for the more important Roman monuments, museums, galleries and public buildings of historic interest. At the time of going to print, every effort has been made to give up-to-date information. However, hours and fees are subject to change at short notice. Consequently, it is important to telephone to be sure of hours of admission. Keep in mind that many Italians take a siesta, usually between the hours of 12.30-16.00. You may find some businesses, museums, etc., closed at this time.

The four major Basilicas of St Peter, St John Lateran, St Mary Major and St Paul Outside the Walls are open from 07.00-19.00 every day. Nearly all other churches close daily from 12.00 or 12.30-15.30 or 16.00. Where there is an admission fee, those under eighteen years of age and EU citizens over sixty years are admitted free: you will be asked to show an official document, such as a passport, or photocopy of a passport. Prices are reduced for students with student cards and for holders of the Council of Europe Cultural Card. You can now purchase a single three-day ticket that gives entrance to four museums and archaeological sites in Rome: the Colosseum, the Palatine, Palazzo Altemps and Palazzo Massimo alle Terme. The ticket costs ITL 20.000 and can be obtained from the ticket office of the participating museums, sites etc. Many museums are free on the last Sunday of the month. In some churches there are coin-operated lights that illuminate works of art. *All museums are closed on Mondays*, except the Vatican Museums, Doria Pamphilj and Palazzo delle Esposizioni.

	Hours	Fee
BATHS OF CARACALLA Via delleTerme di Caracalla, 52 (p. 93)	Summer 09.00-19.00 Winter 09.00-15.00 Sun./Mon. 09.00-14.00	ITL 8.000
CASTEL S. ANGELO Lungotevere Castello, 50 (Borgo) Tel. 06-681-9111 Bus 23, 64, 280 (p. 77)	09.00-21.00 Closed Mondays Sat. 09.00-24.00 Sun. 09-00-20.00	ITL 8.000
CATACOMBS **St Agnes** Via Nomentana, 349 Tel. 06-861-0840 Bus 317, 60, 136, 137, 36, 37, 310 (p. 108)	09.00-12.00; 16.00-18.00 Sun. 16.00-18.00 Closed Mon. afternoon and Sun. morning	ITL 8.000
St Calixtus Via Appia Antica, 110 Tel. 06-513-6725 Bus 660 (p. 95)	08.30-12.00;14.30-17.30 Closed Wednesdays	ITL 8.000
St Domitilla Via delle Sette Chiese, 280 (Ostiense) Tel. 06-511-0342 Bus 671, 714, 716 (p. 95)	08.30-12.00; 14.30-17.30 Closed Tuesdays	ITL 8.000
St Priscilla Via Salaria, 430 (Salaria) Tel. 06-8620-6272 Bus 57, 56, 319 (p. 108)	08.30-12.00; 14.30-17.30 Closed Mondays	ITL 8.000
St Sebastian Via Appia Antica, 136 Tel. 06-788-7035 Bus 660 (p. 95)	08.30-12.00; 14.30-17.30 Closed Sundays	ITL 8.000

VILLA BORGHESE MUSEUM	[Booking obligatory]	ITL 10.000
Piazza Scipione Borghese, 5 (Pinciano)	Booking Fee	ITL 2.000
Villa Borghese	Under 18s/Over 60s	ITL 2.000
Tel. 06-32810	09.00-21.00	
Metro A, Station Spagna	Entry at 09.00, 11.00,	
Bus 116, 910, 53, 52, 19, 30	13.00, 15.00, 17.00, 19.00	
(p. 107)	Sun./Holidays 09.00-19.00	
	Entry at 09.00, 11.00,	
	13.00, 15.00, 17.00	
	Closed Mondays	
CAPITOLINE MUSEUM	09.00-19.00	ITL 5.000
Piazza del Campidoglio	Sun. 09.00-18.45	
Tel. 06-6710-2071/6710-2475	Closed Mondays	
Bus 46, 60, 62, 64, 710, 719, 186		
(p. 87)		
THE COLOSSEUM	09.00-19.00	ITL 10.000
Piazza del Colosseo	Sun./Holidays 09.00-13.00	
(p. 89)		
VILLA GIULIA, ETRUSCAN MUSEUM	09.00-19.00	ITL 8.000
Piazza Villa Giulia, 9	Sun./Holidays 09.00-14.00	
Tel. 06-320-1951	Closed Mondays	
Bus 19, 30, 926, 52		
(p. 107)		
ROMAN FORUM	09.00-19.00	Free
Largo Romolo e Remo 5-6	Sun./Holidays 09.00-14.00	
Piazza S. Maria Nova	Sat./Summer 09.00-24.00	ITL 6.000
(near Arch of Titus)	Daily guided tours in	
(p. 88)	English at 10.45	
TRAJAN'S FORUM (and Markets)	09.00-13.00	
Via IV Novembre	April-Sept 09.00-13.30	
(p. 88)	Thurs., Sat. 09.00-18.00;	
	Sun. 09.00-13.00	
	Closed Mondays	

GALLERY OF THE ACADEMY OF ST LUKE Piazza dell'Accademia di S Luca (near Trevi Fountain) Tel. 06-679-8850	Mon. - Wed. - Fri. 10.00-12.30 Last Sun. of the month	Free
GALLERIA COLONNA Via della Pilotta, 17 Tel. 06-679-4362	Sat. 09.00-13.00	ITL 10.000
GALLERIA DORIA PAMPHILJ Piazza del Collegio Romano, 2 Tel. 06-679-7323 Bus 44, 46, 56, 60, 62, 64, 170, 710	10.00-17.00 Students/Over 60s Tour of Private Apartments 10.30-12.30 Closed Thursdays	ITL 13.000 ITL 5.000 ITL 5.000
GALLERY OF ANCIENT ART – NATIONAL GALLERY (Palazzo Barberini) Via Barberini, 18 Tel. 06-481-4591/482-4184 Metro A, Barberini. Bus 492, 590, 204, 116, 58, 56, 52, 60 (p. 106)	09.00-21.00 Sun./Holidays 09.00-20.00 Sat 09.00-24.00 Closed Mondays	ITL 8.000
GALLERY OF MODERN ART – NATIONAL GALLERY Viale delle Belle Arti 131 Tel. 06-322981 Bus 926, 19, 306	09.00-19.00 Closed Mondays	ITL 8.000
CITY'S GALLERY OF MODERN ART- GALLERIA COMUNALE DI ARTE MODERNA Via Francesco Crispi, 24 Tel. 06-474-2848 Metro A, Barbarini. Bus 52, 53, 56, 58, 58B, 60, 62, 95, 492	09.00-18.30 Sun. 09.00-13.30 Closed Mondays	ITL 10.000 Reduced ITL 5.000

KEATS-SHELLEY HOUSE	Mon.-Fri. 09.00-13.00;	ITL 5.000
Piazza di Spagna, 26	15.00-18.00	
Tel. 06-6784-4235	Sat. 11.00-14.00;	
Metro A, Spagna.	15.00-18.00	
Bus 117	Closed Sund.	
(p. 106)		
MAMERTINE PRISON	09.00-12.00;	An offering
Via San Pietro in Carcere	Summer 14.30-17.00	
(p. 88)	Winter 14.30-18.00	
THE PANTHEON	09.00-16.30	Free
Piazza della Rotonda	Sun. 09.00-13.00	
(p. 100)		
S CLEMENTE	09.00-12.30	ITL 5.000
Via S. Giovanni in Laterano	Sun./Holidays 00.10-12.30;	
(p. 133)	15.00-18.00	

SISTINE CHAPEL (see Vatican Museum)

VATICAN MUSEUMS AND GALLERIES	Oct-June 08.45-13.45	ITL 18.000
Viale del Vaticano	Last entry 12.45	
Tel. 06-6988-4947	July-Sept. 08.45-16.45	
Metro A, Cipro-Musei Vaticani.	Last entry 15.45	
Bus 907, 991, 81, 51, 23, 49, 990, 64	Sat. 08.45-12.45	
(p. 75)	Reduced (Group)	ITL 12.000
	Closed Sun. (except the	
	last Sun. of the month,	
	when admission is free).	
	Closed Feasts (January 6,	
	February 11, May 1,	
	June 29, August 15,	
	November 1, December 8,	
	December 25, Easter Mon.)	

ROME THROUGH THE AGES

Early Rome
According to the well-known legend, Romulus and Remus, the twin sons of a vestal virgin and the god Mars, were abandoned, then subsequently rescued and nurtured by a she-wolf and later adopted by shepherds. As young men they decided to build a new city on the hill known as the Palatine, but they quarrelled over its name and Romulus killed Remus. Romulus then built his new city in 753 BC giving it his own name. Thus says the legend.

The Palatine Hill was certainly inhabited by shepherds in the eighth century BC. The city gradually expanded to occupy the seven well-known hills of Rome: the Capitoline and Palatine, the Quirinal hill which is the site today of the Presidential Palace, the Esquiline and Viminal hills where the Basilica of St Mary Major stands, the Coelian, site of St John Lateran, and the Aventine where Santa Sabina and San Anselmo are located. In the seventh century BC, Etruscan kings from the north established a viable community here, which became a commercial centre with a port on the Tiber. A temple to Jupiter was built and a reclaimed adjoining swamp later became the Roman Forum and marketplace.

The Republic
Tarquin, the seventh and last Etruscan king, was expelled by the Roman patrician (noble) families in 509 BC and a Republic was established. The then existing city of Rome was destroyed by the invasion of the Gauls in 390 BC. Just over a hundred years later, the Romans regrouped and colonised Italy and, by 272 BC, they had conquered all of Italy. In the centuries that followed, the Romans expanded their territorial claim on

the Mediterranean world and, in the famous Punic Wars, they finally destroyed the power of Carthage (Third Punic War, 149-146 BC), and Africa became a Roman province. Through their subsequent victories in the Macedonian Wars, the Romans conquered Greece and its territories in Asia Minor and Julius Caesar conquered France and Gaul (58-53 BC).

The resultant wealth and power of Rome led to political intrigue and divisions in the Senate, with many contenders seeking the ultimate and sole power to rule. Julius Caesar's ambition to be Emperor and his death at the hands of Brutus on 15 March, 44 BC, is an example of this struggle.

Imperial Rome and the Christian Era

The growth in size of the territory of Rome placed great strain on the original Republican form of government. Caesar Augustus (63 BC-14 AD) finally established himself as Emperor in 27 BC. The reign of Augustus saw the beginning of a new epoch in the history of the universe and humankind with the birth of Jesus in Bethlehem, the founder of a new Kingdom whose reign would never end (Luke 2:1) It is, of course, His Jubilee we celebrate in 2000.

The Growth of the Empire

Although the Emperor was the leader (*Princeps*), the state was in fact a sort of quasi Republic in which the Senate still played a vital role. During the reign of Augustus, called the Golden Age, Roman civilisation flourished. One has only to think of Virgil, Livy and Ovid, among others. Augustus added new aqueducts, a new forum, the Ara Pacis and the Pantheon. Following the fire of 64, which destroyed half the city, Nero built the Via Sacra, and a new palace, the Domus Aurea. The Colosseum, begun by Vespasian and finished by Titus, was opened in 80, and could seat more than 50,000 spectators. Succeeding Emperors added new fora, baths and public buildings. In 271 Aurelius began the project of building a wall to encircle the city as a defence against the increasing number of barbarian invasions.

The Persecutions

The city of Rome and its citizens absorbed many forms of religious cults and practices as the empire was extended. Such cults and practices were tolerated as long as the official public religion, of which the emperor was *'Pontifex Maximus'*, the supreme High Priest, was not threatened.

In conscience, the Christians were not able to take part in the worship of the Emperor and in other forms of public worship. They were accused of being disloyal to the Emperor and the State and were thus considered guilty of treason. Some Roman Christians and Jewish Christians who had come to Rome were expelled from the city around the year 49-50. Jews had settled in the Trastevere section of Rome before the Christian era and they were the focus of the first Christians who came to Rome to preach about Jesus.

Following the fire of 64, during the time of Nero, the Christians, who were blamed for the fire, were cruelly persecuted by crucifixion and burning and were even used as bait for wild animals in amphitheatre sports. It is probable that at this time the Apostles Peter and Paul were martyred. During the reign of Domitian (81-96) the Christians were accused of being atheists and they were persecuted, even in the provinces. The next two centuries saw a series of organized persecutions under the reign of Diocletian (284-305) and his successors.

The Edict of Constantine
During the reign of Emperor Constantine I (307-337), Christianity was declared to be the official religion of the Empire and, in the Convention or Edict of Milan in 313, Constantine decreed the policy of universal tolerance and granted equal rights to all religions in the Empire:

> We have long considered that freedom of worship should not be denied. Rather, each person's thought and desires should be granted, thus enabling him to have regard for spiritual things as he chooses. This is why we have given orders that everyone should be allowed to have his own beliefs and worship as he wishes.

The Decline of the Empire
Due to the growing power of the Germanic tribes and the Persians, the Romans were on the defensive during the third and fourth centuries, ceding territory to the invading barbarians in some cases. But the seeds of the demise of the Roman Empire were already sown. Rampant injustices, the unbridled ambition of would-be leaders, the decline of the role and rule of law, growing immorality, and the excesses of rulers were factors which combined in time to weaken the spirit and power of Rome. With the final invasions of the barbarians, the Empire began to crumble. The Goths, under Alaric, began the conquest of the Empire, sacking Rome in 410. In 455, the Vandal, Gaiseric, destroyed Rome. Finally, the western Empire became part of the kingdom of the first barbarian king of Italy, Odoacer, who deposed the Emperor Romulus Augustulus in 476.

The Papal States
After the seat of the Western Empire had moved from Rome to Ravenna

in 404, the Popes gradually took over much of the administrative functions of the civil administration of Rome, while remaining loyal to the Emperor. In the eighth century, Italy was invaded by the Longobards, who established strong states at Pavia and Benevento, north and south of Rome. The Byzantine Emperors retained a foothold in Ravenna and Rome. The corridor joining these two outposts became the Papal States. Pope Stephen II (752-757) was assisted by the Frankish King, Pepin the Short, who defeated the Longobards and established the Pope's temporal sovereignty. In 800, Pope St Leo III crowned Pepin's son, Charlemagne, as Holy Roman Emperor in the Basilica of St Peter. Early medieval Popes successfully asserted their supremacy over the civil power.

Avignon

In 1309, Rome had become unsafe because of the internecine strife of the local barons. When a French Cardinal was elected Pope at a conclave held in Perugia in 1309, he was crowned in Lyon and remained in France, eventually establishing the Papal residence in Avignon in the South of France. His successors continued to reside there until Pope Gregory XI returned to Rome in 1378. A number of Cardinals did not recognise the change and elected a series of antipopes in the Great Western Schism which lasted until the election of Pope Martin V in 1417.

Return of Popes to Rome and the Renaissance

On their return to Rome from Avignon in 1378, successive Popes established a system of administration to govern the city, which had fallen into decay. Many new buildings, a new evolving style and the great Renaissance artists under the patronage of Popes Alexander VI, Julius II, Leo X and Clement VII, all contributed to the city of Rome becoming a centre of great culture.

The Early Renaissance, prefigured in the work of the great artist Giotto (1266-1337), also known as 'the father of Italian art', sought to portray a sense of a concrete realism and accuracy. A new humanism was apparent in the growing number of secular subjects depicted in the various art forms. Some well-known artists of this period are the painter Masaccio (1401-1428) who worked in Pisa and Florence, the Florentine Dominican, Blessed Fra Angelico (1400-1455), known for his glorious tones, who, we are told, prayed as he painted, and Sandro Botticelli (1444-1510), known for his enigmatic paintings such as the allegorical *Primavera* and *The Birth of Venus*.

In Rome, many buildings were gradually restored after years of neglect while many new buildings, such as the Palazzo Farnese (1450) and Palazzo della Cancelleria (1483), now the site of the Vatican tribunals, including the Rota, gave concrete form to the new spirit. The area of the city south of the Corso Vittorio Emanuele reflects this great blossoming of the Renaissance. The Campo dei Fiori and the Via Giulia were centres of artistic and cultural life.

During the High Renaissance, which began in Italy in the 1490s, among the great artists noted for their precision, realism and objectivity, were Leonardo da Vinci (1452-1519), Bramante (1444-1514), whose designs and buildings epitomised the harmony of the Renaissance; Michelangelo (1475-1564) who developed the spirit of the Renaissance to extraordinary levels of accomplishment in his native Florence and in his adopted city of Rome, Raphael (1483-1520) who would influence art and architecture for centuries to come, and Titian (1488-1567), student of Bellini, whose *Christ appearing to Mary Magdalen* and later works display a superb technique.

Despite the sack of Rome in 1527 by the German imperial troops of Charles V, and the tensions and divisions caused by the Protestant Reformation, the splendour of Rome continued. With the help and support of the Spanish royal house the papacy and the curia ruled the city.

Rome and the Baroque

In a city of rich and poor, of splendour and abject poverty, the Popes continued to promote culture and the arts, and Rome became the centre of what is known as the Baroque period, which began to develop at the dawn of the seventeenth century. The survival and confidence of the Catholic Church after the Protestant Reformation, and the energetic Counter Reformation, called forth the characteristics of realism, emotional force, and spiritual intensity in art, literature, architecture and in civil society. Caravaggio (1573-1610), with his light and darkness, good and evil, as seen in *Bacchus*, and the then shocking *The Death of the Virgin*, would lead the way to greater realism in art. The 'divine' genius of Guido Reni (1575-1642) and Guercino (1591-1666) are supreme examples of the high emotion, drama, realism and magnificent colours of Italian Baroque painting, as can been seen in their respective works, *Susanna and the Elders* and *Christ and the Woman taken in Adultery*.

The new Basilica of St Peter, begun in 1506 by Bramante (1444-1514) at the request of Julius II, who decided on a new building rather than a reconstruction of the existing structure, was consecrated by Pope Urban VIII in 1626. The Popes, such as Sixtus V and Urban VIII, commissioned many of the great Baroque buildings of the late sixteenth and seventeenth centuries. Papal patronage promoted the genius of such artists as Gian Lorenzo Bernini (1598-1680), the great sculptor and architect, Pietro da Cortona (1596-1669), whose frescoes in the Palazzo

Barberini established him as a major exponent of the Baroque style, Borromini (1599-1667), whose work in the Church of St Charles at Quattro Fontane demonstrates his late Baroque skills. The Jesuit church, the Gesú, completed in 1575, is often said to be the first and most influential building in the Baroque style. Carlo Maderna (1556-1629), who worked on St Peter's and its façade, was another early influential builder in the Baroque school.

The Decline of Papal Temporal Power

The period from the French Revolution in 1789 to the Unification of Italy in 1870 was one of increasing tension and unrest for both the city of Rome and the Papacy. It was a time of foreign occupation, plots, political assassinations and, for the Popes, there was the threat of physical danger. Three Popes were forced out or fled the Vatican: Pius VI in 1799, Pius VII from 1808 until the defeat of Napoleon in 1814, and Pius IX in 1848, when he fled Rome after the assassination of his chief minister and head of police, Pellegrino Rossi. The Pope only returned the following year thanks to help from the French troops who defeated Giuseppe Garibaldi and his supporters after several months of fighting in and around Rome.

From the Papal States to the Republic of Italy

The tense months of the Roman revolution in 1849 were only the beginning of the efforts of Garibaldi and Cavour to put an end to the temporal power of the Papacy in their struggle to unite Italy. But the Kingdom of Italy, which was proclaimed in 1861 under King Victor Emmanuel, was not prepared to take on the fight with the Papacy while it was still protected by the French. It was not until 1870, when Napoleon III was defeated in the Franco-Prussian war and the French were withdrawing from Rome, that the Italian army, under General Cadorna, breached the city's walls at Porta Pia. Pius IX withdrew to the Vatican, and Rome became the capital of a united Italy the following year. It would be another sixty years before, under the terms of the 1929 Lateran treaties, some measure of temporal power was once again restored to the Papacy.

The immediate aftermath of the Unification of Italy saw an enormous building boom in the new capital city. The area around the Vatican known as Prati (green fields), the Palace of Justice near Castel S. Angelo, the Tiber embankments, the Victor Emmanuel Monument in Piazza Venezia, Via Nazionale, all stem from this period. The walls of the ghetto, where the Jews were confined and subject to curfew from the sixteenth century onwards, were also torn down during this time and the present synagogue was erected on a part of the site in the 1880s.

Another period of development for the city came during the two decades of Fascist rule, from the mid 1920s to Italy's entry into the Second World War on the side of the Germans in 1940. Some of the most obvious signs of the Fascist period are Via della Conciliazione leading up to the Basilica of St Peter, Via dei Fori Imperiale which runs from Piazza Venezia to the Colosseum and the suburb of EUR (see p. 124)

During World War II, Rome, unlike many other Italian cities, suffered only slight bomb damage due to the intervention of Pope Pius XII. The city was finally liberated from the Germans in 1944. In 1946, Italians voted narrowly against the monarchy and in favour of a Republic.

GREAT JUBILEE YEAR 2000

Origins of the Holy Year

Among the early Christian pilgrims to Rome were the Apostles Peter and Paul, who came to plead their causes before Caesar Augustus. Paul came to Rome due to the express wish of Jesus: 'That night the Lord stood before him and said, "Keep up your courage! For just as you have testified for me in Jerusalem, so you must bear witness also in Rome".' (cf. Acts 23:11). Following their deaths, the tombs of the Apostles in Rome became centres of pilgrimage, a tradition which received a new focus and impetus when, in the year 1300, Pope Boniface VIII proclaimed a 'Holy Year', a special celebration of peace, reconciliation and forgiveness. This celebration was in a direct line of tradition with the well-known biblical celebration every fifty years of the 'Jubilee Year'. The word 'jubilee', which is used for the Holy Year, stems from the Hebrew word '*yobel*', a ram's horn, which is the word for the trumpet which was sounded in the Temple at Jerusalem to announce to all the beginning of the Jubilee Year (cf. Lev 25:2-12).

Purpose

The Jubilee Year was a call to imitate God in his goodness and mercy towards his people, a call to care for the earth, to allow the land to rest so that it would recover its vitality and fertility, a time to forgive debts – especially those of the poor – a time to restore ill-gotten goods, a time of reconciliation, pardon and justice, with special care for the weak and poor. The Jubilee Year was a more solemn celebration of the 'sabbatical year', which was observed by the Jews every seven years, during which the earth was left fallow and slaves were set free. The Jubilee Year was a time for recognising that creation and all its ecosystems, as well as all economic goods, belonged to God, a loving and compassionate Father who should be loved and imitated in return. The love of the Father is valid only if it is shown by caring for His creation and by the practical love of neighbour, especially the weak, the poor, the oppressed and the marginalised. When Jesus, filled with the Spirit of the Lord, spoke in the synagogue of Nazareth (cf. Lk 4:16-3), declaring he had come 'to bring good news to the oppressed, to bind up the brokenhearted, to proclaim liberty to captives, and release to the prisoners; to proclaim the year of the Lord's favour,' he was referring to this ancient biblical celebration which he would renew, fulfil and make totally new.

Modern Structure

Pope Boniface VIII declared that a universal Holy Year should be celebrated every one hundred years, stipulating that in order to receive the indulgences and forgiveness of sins, visits – thirty for Romans and fifteen for foreigners – were to be made to the Roman Basilicas of the two Apostles, St Peter and St Paul. In fact, the next ordinary Holy Year was celebrated in the year 1350, and this was followed by an extraordinary Holy Year which was announced by Pope Boniface IX and celebrated in 1390. The Basilicas to be visited were those of St Peter, St Paul, St John Lateran and St Mary Major. Pope Martin V proclaimed a Holy Year in 1425 and Pope Sixtus IV established, beginning in the year 1475, that a Holy Year should be celebrated every twenty-five years. This arrangement of proclaiming a Holy Year every twenty-five years has continued since then, with the exception of the years 1800 and 1850.

APOSTOLIC LETTER OF POPE JOHN PAUL II
ANNOUNCING THE GREAT JUBILEE YEAR 2000

With the Apostolic Letter *Tertio Millennio Adveniente*, 10 November 1994, Pope John Paul II announced the celebration of the Holy Year 2000, calling it the 'Great Jubilee'. The Pope considers the holding of the Second Vatican Council (1962-1965) and such events as the recent Regional Synods of Bishops, the publication of Papal documents, the Papal Journeys and Congresses as part of the remote and proximate preparations for the celebration of the Great Jubilee 2000. What follows is a summary of some of the more important points of the Pope's Letter.

In Christianity, time has a fundamental importance. With the birth of Jesus – the Son of God made flesh, the Lord of time, the 'beginning and the end'– time becomes a dimension of the eternal God.

Jesus, in his words and deeds, is the fulfilment of all the biblical

Jubilees, which foretold and anticipated the total freedom for all with the coming of the Messiah. Thus, leaving aside the question of exact dating, the passing of two thousand years since the birth of Jesus, Son of God and Son of Mary, is an extraordinary event for the whole of humanity: it is indeed a 'Great Jubilee'. For this reason Pope John Paul II invites all Christians and humankind to share with joy the salvation brought by Christ. The Pope proposes two phases of preparation for the Great Jubilee.

Phase One:
The Christological Significance of the Jubilee Year 2000

The first phase would help people realise the deep Christological significance of the Year 2000 in human history. The Jubilee celebration would confirm the Christians of today in their *faith* in God who has revealed himself in Christ, sustain their *hope* which reaches out in expectation of eternal life, and rekindle their *charity* in active service to their brothers and sisters. The Jubilee is meant to be 'a great *prayer of praise and thanksgiving*, especially for the *gift of the Incarnation of the Son of God and the Redemption* which he accomplished.' In reality, the joy of every Jubilee celebration is a joy that is '*based upon the forgiveness of sins, the joy of conversion*,' and a turning away from the sinfulness of ways of acting 'which were truly *forms of counter-witness and scandal.*' Among the sins which call for true repentance and conversion are those '*which have been detrimental to the unity willed by God for his People*,' a unity so often shattered in certain centuries by '*intolerance and even the use of violence*,' by '*grave forms of injustice and exclusion*.' This quest for unity calls for a serious examination of conscience and unceasing prayer as it is fundamentally a gift of the Holy Spirit.

Phase Two:
The Preparation for the Celebration of the Jubilee Year 2000

The second phase of preparation for the celebration of the Great Jubilee has been the span of three years from 1997 to 1999. With Christ, the Son of God made man, the focal point, the thematic structure of the preparation period was both *Christological* and *Trinitarian.*

Year One: 1997 'Jesus Christ, the one Saviour of the world, yesterday, today and for ever' (cf. Heb 13:18).

With a renewed interest in the Bible and the celebration of the Word of God, Christians endeavour to strengthen their faith in Jesus as the one Saviour and to become true witnesses of the Gospel, striving to have '*a true longing for holiness*, a deep desire for conversion and personal renewal in a context of ever more intense prayer and of solidarity with one's neighbour, especially the most needy.' Such a genuine renewal inevitably leads to a deep contemplation of the Divine Motherhood of Mary in whose womb the Word became flesh and who is our *model of faith*.

Year Two: 1998 'The Holy Spirit'
The Incarnation was accomplished '*by the power of the Holy Spirit*,' the source of every gift that comes from God. Thus, it is only '*in the Spirit*' that Christians can prepare for the new millennium, seeking a renewed appreciation of the activity and presence of the Spirit who is 'the One who builds the Kingdom of God within the course of history and prepares its full manifestation in Jesus Christ.' Recourse to Mary, who was always open to the promptings of the Spirit, is a necessary part of renewing our awareness of the Spirit still very active in the world.

Year Three: 1999 'God the Father'
In the final year of preparation, Christians are called to have the mind of Christ and to see all things in the perspective '*of the Father who is in heaven*' (cf. Matt 5:45), the Father who sent the Lord and to whom he has returned. The whole of the Christian life is like 'a great *pilgrimage to the house of the Father*, whose unconditional love for every human creature, and in particular for the "prodigal son" (cf. Lk 15:11-32), we discover anew each day. This pilgrimage takes place in the heart of each person, extends to the believing community and then reaches out to the whole of humanity.' The sense of being on a 'journey to the Father' should inspire all to undertake a pilgrimage, a journey of authentic '*conversion*', which includes reconciliation with God and humankind, and also involves a commitment of service, a commitment to justice and peace in a world torn apart 'by so many conflicts and intolerable social and economic inequalities.' Imbued with the spirit of the Book of Leviticus (cf. 25:8-12), 'Christians will have to raise their voice on behalf of all the poor of the world,' proposing the Jubilee as an appropriate time to give thought, among other things, to cancelling outright, the international debt which seriously threatens the future of many nations. The Pope states that the Jubilee also offers 'an opportunity for reflecting on other challenges of our time, such as the difficulties of dialogue between different cultures and the problems connected with respect for women's rights and the promotion of the family and marriage.' Two aspects of modern life, '*meeting the challenge of secularism and dialogue with the great religions*,' should be the concern of all. A civilization which is technologically very sophisticated but tends to keep God at a distance 'must be countered by *the civilization of love*, founded on the universal values of peace,

solidarity, justice and liberty, which find their full attainment in Christ.' The Pope insists that the Jubilee 2000 celebrations are a time of special grace for the whole of humanity.

Key Themes of the Great Jubilee 2000

The aim of the actual celebration of the Great Jubilee 2000 is *'to give glory to the Trinity'*, from whom everything in the world and in history comes and to whom everything returns. This mystery is the focus of the three years of immediate preparation: 'from Christ and through Christ, in the Holy Spirit, to the Father.' The Pope insists that the Jubilee 2000 is a time of special grace of the Lord for the Church and for the whole of humanity. Special emphasis is placed on certain aspects of the celebration: *Conversion, Reconciliation, Jubilee Indulgences and Charity towards the needy, Inter-religious Dialogue, Ecumenism,* the *Eucharist,* the *Family, Youth* and the *new Martyrs.*

Conversion, Reconciliation, Jubilee Indulgences and Charity

A Jubilee is a time of special grace and joy. The special joy of every Jubilee is a joy based upon conversion and forgiveness of sins, and reconciliation with God and with our brothers and sisters. As 'prodigal' sons and daughters of a loving Father who reveals himself in Christ, all are asked to seek God's infinite mercy and pardon. The embrace of a loving Father will be the gift we receive for our pilgrimage of sorrow and reconciliation. The humble recognition and confession of our personal and communitarian faults and sins, the reception of the Sacrament of Reconciliation and the celebration of the Eucharist restore us to unity with Jesus and His Church. In addition, prayers offered for the Pope's intentions (ending with the 'Our Father', the 'Creed' and a prayer to Our Lady), accompanied by works of penance and charity, especially towards the poor and needy, and a visit to one of the basilicas in Rome, gain an *indulgence*, the remission of the temporal punishment due to our sins. The indulgence may also be applied to the dead. To gain an indulgence it is sufficient during the Jubilee Year to participate in a liturgical celebration – Morning Prayer or Evening Prayer of the Church, the Stations of the Cross, the Rosary, a visit to a basilica with Eucharistic adoration – concluding with the prescribed prayers.

The designated Basilicas in Rome are the four Patriarchal Basilicas, namely, the Basilica of St Peter in the Vatican (see p. 63), the Basilica of St John Lateran (see p. 83) the Basilica of St Mary Major (see p. 79) and the Basilica of St Paul Outside the Walls (see p. 96). On the special occasion of the Jubilee the following are also designated places for gaining an indulgence: the Basilica of the Holy Cross in Jerusalem (see p. 84), the

Basilica of St Lawrence in Campo Verano (see p. 65), the Shrine of Our Lady of Divine Love (see p. 168) and the Christian Catacombs.

A sign of the mercy of God is the sign of charity which opens our eyes to the needs of others, especially the poor and excluded. Extreme poverty is a source of violence, bitterness and scandal: to seek to eradicate it is to do the work of justice and therefore the work of peace, integral elements of the Gospel of Jesus. During the Jubilee Year all acts of charity and service to the sick, the imprisoned, the elderly living alone, the handicapped, etc., are elements of a pilgrimage to meet Christ: 'Then the King will say to those at his right hand, "Come, you that are blessed by my Father, inherit the kingdom prepared for you from the foundation of the world; for I was hungry and you gave me food, I was thirsty and you gave me something to drink, I was a stranger and you welcomed me, I was naked and you gave me clothing, I was sick and you took care of me, I was in prison and you visited me."' (Mt 25:34-36). With the appropriate prayers these acts of charity are occasions for receiving an indulgence. All practices of fasting, alms-giving, and activities of personal sacrifice for others are ways of benefitting fully from the graces of the Jubilee.

Christian, Jewish, Moslem and Inter-Religious Dialogue
The Great Jubilee of the Year 2000 will be celebrated in Rome and in all the local churches throughout the world. It will have two main focal points: Rome, with the See of the successor of St Peter, the Vicar of Christ on earth, and Jerusalem, where Jesus Christ, the Son of God made man was born of the Virgin Mary. The Jubilee Year will be celebrated with equal solemnity and dignity in Rome and Jerusalem. Jerusalem is the 'Holy City in the Holy Land, where Jesus was born in Bethlehem and where God revealed himself to the Jewish people. This is 'the promised Land' which is also sacred to the followers of Islam. A very important aim of the Jubilee Year is the promotion of mutual dialogue so that one day, Jews, Christians, and Moslems 'will exchange the greeting of peace in Jerusalem.'

The Calendar of the Jubilee 2000 emphasises the importance of inter-faith dialogue by setting aside Sunday, 11 June 2000, as a day of special prayer for the promotion of collaboration among the different religions. In Rome, this day of prayer will be centred on the Basilica of St Peter, but it will be also celebrated, as is the case with all the themes during the Jubilee, throughout the world. Tuesday, 3 October 2000 is a day especially devoted to Jewish-Christian dialogue.

Ecumenism

Another important aspect of the Jubilee Year will be the Ecumenical dimension whereby all the baptised and the faithful of the different Churches and Ecclesial Communities will unite 'in listening to the Spirit that we shall be able to show forth visibly in full communion the grace of divine adoption which springs from Baptism: all of us children of the one Father.' The Holy Father's wish is that the two thousandth anniversary of the central mystery of the Christian faith, the coming of the Son of God among us as a man, may be a journey of reconciliation and a sign of true hope for all who look to Christ.

With the opening of the Holy Door in the Basilica of St. Paul Outside the Walls on Tuesday, 18 January 2000, the Week of Prayer for Christian Unity begins with a special Ecumenical Celebration in the basilica. There will be a similar celebration on Tuesday, 25 January, at the conclusion of the Week of Prayer.

Eucharistic Congress

Christ is the perfect way to the Father and the International Eucharistic Congress in Rome during the Great Jubilee Year will highlight the Eucharistic presence of Christ, the Son of God and Son of Mary. The Congress will begin in the Basilica of St John Lateran on Trinity Sunday, 18 June 2000, and will conclude the following Sunday.

The Family

During the Year of the Family in 1994, the Church emphasised the dignity of marriage and the family in society. The celebration of the Christian family is closely connected with the mystery celebrated in the Jubilee 2000 celebations. We celebrate the very history of humanity when we celebrate the begining of the Third Millennium of the mystery of the Incarnation, God becoming man in a human family, the Holy Family. The Jubilee celebrations of the Family will be celebrated on 14 and 15 October 2000, when the Pope will meet with families from many parts of the world. On Sunday 15 October the Pope will preside at the celebration of the Sacrament of Matrimony in St Peter's Square.

Youth

A celebration of great importance is the fifteenth gathering of the youth of the world for the special celebration to be held between Tuesday 15 August and Sunday 20 August 2000. Recognising that the future of the world and the Church belongs to the younger generation, the Pope says that Christ expects great things from young people, as he did from the young person who asked him, 'Teacher, what good deed must I do to have eternal life?'(Mt. 19:16). The young people who keep asking questions and searching for Christ today are those who will prolong his presence in the new millennium.

Martyrs of the 20th Century

With the celebration of the Jubilee in mind, Pope John Paul II makes frequent references to the 'new martyrs' – Protestant, Orthodox and Catholic – who have given their lives for the Christian faith in the twentieth century. The Pope sees them as a 'light' for humankind and as 'saints' who unite the divided Christian churches and communities. There will be a special ecumenical celebration to honour these Christian martyrs on 7 May 2000, in the Colosseum, a place that evokes many memories of Christian suffering.

CHRISTIAN PILGRIMAGE

The documents of the Second Vatican Council, held in Rome in the early 1960s, repeatedly refer to the Church, the assembly of the followers of Christ, as the *Pilgrim People of God*. History makes many references to the notion of pilgrimage. A religious pilgrimage is a journey to a sacred shrine or sanctuary or a place that is 'holy' for a religious reason. Such journeys are a part of most religions, cults and beliefs. People went on journeys of thanksgiving, with offerings of goods and stock, to places where the gods were said to live. The practice of sacred journeys is found many times in the Old Testament, which recounts the journey of the Hebrew people in the desert on their way to, and taking possession of, the Promised Land. The passages describing the celebration of the main feasts of the Israelites (for example, Ex 23:14-19; Deut 16 *passim*; Ps 42, 43), and the historian Josephus (ca. 37-101 AD), speak of the large crowds gathered in Jerusalem to celebrate the Feast of Yahweh (God the Father).

Mary and Joseph went to Jerusalem every year, bringing the child Jesus with them when he was twelve years of age (cf. Lk 2:41-42). The Evangelist St Luke, in his version of the Gospel, speaks of the life and ministry of Jesus as one long journey from his infancy in Galilee to his passion, death, resurrection and ascension, the return to the Father being the end of his pilgrimage. Every Christian pilgrimage is an association with Jesus on that journey. The institution of the Eucharist took place when Jesus and his Apostles were on their annual Passover pilgrimage to Jerusalem and it can be said that the Eucharist was the culmination of Christ's pilgrimage on earth.

The followers of Jesus in the first Christian centuries went on pilgrimages to venerate the places in the Holy Land made holy by the life of Jesus in order to venerate Christ, to do penance, to seek forgiveness, blessings and favours. Constantine's promulgation of peace (*Edict of Milan*, 313) and the rebuilding of Jerusalem, with the establishment of shrines and sanctuaries in places and sites associated with the life of Jesus, led to a fostering of the notion of the Christian on pilgrimage.

Pilgrims also went to places made holy by the saints, especially the martyrs. Writings in the catacombs indicate that pilgrims also came to Rome in the first centuries, mainly to pray at the tombs of the martyred Apostles, Saints Peter and Paul, and to meet and pray with St Peter's successor, the Pope. The capture of Jerusalem by non-Christian rulers, with the consequent difficulties of making a pilgrimage to the holy places, resulted in other centres becoming more the focus of pilgrims, and Rome became particularly popular.

In later centuries, in addition to Jerusalem and Rome, many local shrines and sanctuaries became the focal points of pilgrimages. With the discovery of the supposed tomb of the Apostle James, the site in Compostela became popular as a place of pilgrimage. Some other famous centres were Tours in France (it is said that St Patrick spent four years with St Martin in Tours); and Canterbury, in honour of St Thomas Beckett (1171). In modern times, many Marian apparitions and devotional traditions have given rise to famous and popular pilgrimages such as Guadalupe in Mexico (sixteenth century), La Salette (1846), Lourdes (1858), Knock (1879) and Fatima (1917).

The Irish in Rome through the Ages

Though information is scarce, there is evidence that the Irish soon took to heart St Patrick's advice to be both Christians and Romans. In the Middle Ages, Europe was crisscrossed with an extensive network of roads, paths and treks leading to the places of Christian pilgrimages. One of the principal and most frequented roads from the north was that which led from Canterbury to Rome. From the sixth century there has been an unending line of pilgrims on these routes leading to Rome. The pilgrim journey was long and tiring, as it was travelled mainly on foot and often in difficult places. Hospices were built and maintained along the major routes to shelter the tired pilgrim. Among the hospices founded on the route to Rome were St Fiacre's at Breuil (ca. 650) and St Brigid's at Piacenza (ca. 850). St Colman resided in Rome in the early ninth century while promoting the veneration of St Brigid. Donnchadh, the deposed King of Munster and son of the High King Brian Boru, came to Rome in 1064 and is buried in the Church of S. Stefano Rotondo (see p. 90). There was an Irish monastic foundation near S. Stefano Rotondo which was called Trinità degli Scotti (*Trinity of the Irish*). Mentioned as one of the more important abbeys of Rome in the twelfth century, the names of some of the monks were Eoghan, Columbanus, Nicholas, Finian. In all probability the abbey would have been a welcome refuge for many tired pilgrims from Ireland. St Malachy, Archbishop of Armagh, visited Rome in 1140 and St Laurence O'Toole, Archbishop of Dublin, was present at the Third Lateran Council (1179), while eighteen Irish bishops attended the Fourth Lateran Council (1215-1216). Irish pilgrims during the first Holy Years, 1300-1500, probably stayed in hospices. In 1534, Archdeacon Charles Reynolds of Kells, Co.

Meath, arrived in Rome to ask Pope Paul III to lift the excommunication of Silken Thomas, whose followers had murdered Archbishop Allen, Archbishop of Dublin. Reynolds died in Rome and his tombstone is in the cloisters of the Basilica of St John Lateran.

The Formation of Priests

Because of the suppression of the Catholic Church in Ireland and the imposition of the penal laws, many efforts were made in Rome and other European cities to form Irish seminarians who would return to minister in Ireland as priests. There were some Irish seminarians for the diocesan priesthood studying in Rome at the German College in the late sixteenth and early seventeenth centuries. In 1625, Luke Wadding, the Waterford-born Franciscan, founded St Isidore's, the Irish Franciscan College at Via degli Artisti 41, for the formation of Irish Franciscans (see p. 129). Three years later, with the help of Cardinal Ludovico Ludovisi, he founded the Irish College so that seminarians could be formed for the Irish secular clergy (see p. 129). The first Augustinian foundation for formation was in 1656 (see p. 134) and the Dominicans arrived in 1677 (see p. 133).

The students who came to Rome were fascinated by the city and its culture. It enriched many and, unfortunately, contributed also to the vaults that house the bones of others. The archives of the Irish College contain the oaths of many early students, who promised in writing, under God, to return to work in Ireland rather than succumb to the attraction of remaining in Rome. Ireland and many other parts of the globe have benefited over the centuries by the witness of those who studied here and then returned home or went on mission to foreign lands. Some gave witness to their faith by their deaths. The majority gave life to the Church in many lands, enhanced diverse and distant cultures and contributed to the development of many continents and countries.

Oliver Plunkett (1629-1681) from Oldcastle, Co. Meath, a student of the Irish College, became the martyred Archbishop of Armagh and a canonised saint. Charles Meehan, the Franciscan, is a beatified Irish martyr. The Augustinian, James Doyle (1786-1834), became the famous bishop of Kildare and Leighlin, JKL. Francis O'Molloy OFM, published the first grammar book printed in Irish. Together with Luke Wadding (1588-1657), Anthony Hickey (1586-1641) and John Punch (1599-1661), these-seventeenth-century Irish Franciscans attracted students from other Roman colleges to the halls of St Isidore's and made it a noted centre of learning.

Columba Marmion (1858-1923), whose cause is being promoted, was a Dublin student at the Irish College, and became the well-known Benedictine spiritual writer and Abbot of Maredsous. The Dominican

Joseph Mullooly (1812-1880), the amateur archaeologist from Lanesboro, Co. Longford, began the remarkable excavations at San Clemente. Monsignor Padraic de Brún, scholar and wit, became the President of UCG. James Gould OSA, became Bishop of Melbourne, Luke Concannon OP (1747-1810) was appointed first Bishop of New York. In recent times, Archbishop Seàn Brady, Archbishop of Armagh, was a student at, and former Rector of, the Irish College. Martin Nolan OSA was the first Irish General of the Augustinian Order. Cardinal Michael Browne OP and Damian Byrne OP were Masters General of the Dominican Order.

From Africa to Australia, Antrim to America, students who walked these streets of Rome and prepared for the priesthood in the city have served the Church and witnessed to the greatness of the spirit of Ireland. Today the inheritors of this great tradition still follow their paths. Reduced in number, only the Irish College and St Isidore's continue the great presence in Rome.

The Earls of Tyrone and Tyrconnel

A major historic event in the early seventeenth century was the arrival of the defeated Northern Earls, Hugh O'Neill of Tyrone, and Roderick O'Donnell of Tyrconnel, with their families and followers. The distinguished exiles were met at the Milvian Bridge on 30 April 1608, and many honours were accorded to them in Rome, where they lived in a residence made available to them by Pope Paul V. Tragedy soon struck both families, however. Hugh O'Neill's son died and then malaria caused the deaths of two of O'Donnell's sons in 1608. The three are buried in the Spanish church of S. Pietro in Montorio. Hugh O'Neill, who died in 1616, is also buried there (see p. 120). The President of the Republic of Ireland, Mary McAleese, visited the burial places of the Earls in 1999.

The Irish Battalion in the Papal Forces of 1860

In 1859, a strong national movement towards unity, the *Risorgimento*, took command in the north of Italy under Victor Emmanuel, King of Piedmont. This was the first step towards the formation of a united Italy. Between the Papal States and Piedmont lay the central states of Tuscany, Modena and Parma. All three opted to join with Piedmont as did a part of the Papal States, a move which was the beginning of the end of the Papal States. Before the end of 1859 the north Italian rule extended south into the Papal States and with Napoleon III and Cavour working together as 'accomplices', as Cavour put it, the intention was to eventually rule the entire country, something which would be impossible without conquering the Papal States, which lay across the centre of it.

Despite very limited resources and manpower, Pope Pius IX felt constrained to defend the Papal States. He appealed to the Catholic nations for soldiers and arms to bolster his own army in defending the boundaries of the Papal States. During the early months of 1860, volunteers from many nations began to arrive to form an army of separate corps which were united by the cause of the Church and of Rome. An Irish brigade arrived in the summer of 1860, one of the last of the 'Irish Brigades' which served abroad in so many countries. Though many in Ireland favoured the cause of Italian liberation and unity, those who volunteered felt the call of loyalty to the Church and the Pope, especially a Pope who had sought to help Ireland in her hour of famine and need.

The Irish volunteers came from a country where the Catholic Church was suppressed – in 1560 the Act of Supremacy had made Queen Elizabeth I the ruler of the Church in Ireland. It was a country that had experienced the harsh code of penal laws for a long time, Catholic Emancipation only being granted as recently as 1829. During the dark days of the previous century the supportive role of the Church had became an integral part of nationhood, culture and creed. In 1847, Ireland was blighted and devastated by the Famine. Pope Pius IX immediately sent personal funds to help the suffering and urged bishops and the faithful to subscribe to the relief work. The famous preacher, Father Ventura, preached a moving sermon in the Church of Sant'Andrea della Valle on 24 January 1847, to elicit help for Ireland. (Father Ventura was to preach the panegyric at the packed funeral service for Daniel O'Connell a few months later in the same church).

In Ireland, propaganda and mass meetings were quickly organised and, within a month, the first group of volunteers, representing all strata of society, had departed for Italy to fight for the Pope on two pennies and a halfpenny per day, plus their keep. By the end of July 1860 there was a battalion of eight companies with about eleven hundred volunteers known as the Battalion of St Patrick. Four companies were posted to Ancona in the north, and four to Spoleto.

The volunteers from Ireland returned home after the defeat of the badly organised and poorly provisioned Papal army: none had been away for more than four and a half months. Many joined other armies and some became officers and fought in other wars such as the American Civil War.

Irish Artists in Rome

Rome, the cradle of artists, inevitably drew kindred spirits from all over Europe to its *botteghe*. The Grand Tours undertaken at the end of the eighteenth century provided them with a rich variety of work and attracted many to the banks of the Tiber. A significant number of Irish were numbered among them. Generally, together with the English, they congregated in clusters, lived in poor conditions and formed what was called the *ghetto degli Inglesi* near the Piazza di Spagna. Here they frequented the Café degli Inglesi on the west side of the Piazza. Some lived near the café and worked on the Via Sistina, at the top of the Spanish steps. Others lived in the Parish of S. Lorenzo in Lucina and in the surrounding areas.

During the second half of the eighteenth century, Irish artists included painters, sculptors and art dealers. Names of painters such as James Ennis, Robert Crone and James Trotter appear in the *Stato delle Anime* of the various parishes. Some came here by chance, others by choice or commission. The Dublin Society arranged for a number to come to Rome. These included the sculptor George Crawley and the painters James Barry, Matthew Nulry and Robert Crone. It is almost certain that they all lived and died in Rome. Timothy Colopy, the Limerick painter, whose works hang in St John's Cathedral and at the Augustinian Priory, studied in Rome in the late eighteenth century and then returned to Ireland.

Of the Irish art dealers, Thomas Jenkins was the best known, acting as a banker as well as a dealer. He is reputed to have sold Bernini's *Neptune* to Sir Joshua Reynolds. Another Irishman, Tresham, is said to have made a vast profit from the Bishop of Derry, by selling paintings which he bought for fifty crowns. Letters from another dealer, Robert Fagan, show that he acquired many paintings, including a Venus by Titian, and shipped them at great profit from Leghorn to England. Gifted with craft as well as skill, many of the Irish were also self-appointed guides to the 'Grand Tourists' of the day. One who lacked these qualities was described as 'not being of that oily supple disposition necessary to the profession and disdaining the little Arts, etc., and pretensions to ancient Erudition that most of these gentlemen assume – he did not find much employment in that line.' Others were also less fortunate and it is recorded that Richard O'Mooney, having been at a coffee house in Piazza di Spagna, was found dead near the terrace of Trinità de' Monti, with his legs and arms broken and his skull fractured. Living in poor conditions conscious of their dependence on patrons and luck, a good deal of tension existed between artists at that time and, unfortunately, contributed to their hard life.

In the second half of the eighteenth century, many of the artists living in Rome died there. Christopher Hewetsome, who studied at the Academia S. Luca, and whose work included a bust of Frederick Hervey,

Bishop of Derry, died and is buried in an unmarked grave in the English Cemetery. Jonathon Skelton, Matthew Nulry, James Durno and some others certainly died in Rome too and are buried in unknown graves. James Forrester, however, had a monument erected to him in Santa Maria del Popolo, records of which still exist.

While the second half of the eighteenth century probably saw the greatest number of Irish artists in Rome, the nineteenth century artists included Henry Jones Thaddeus, the Cork-born painter, and the sculptor John Hogan, born at Tallow, Co. Waterford. Thaddeus worked in Florence and Rome. His portrait of Pope Leo XIII was the first papal portrait by an Irish artist. Hogan lived in Rome for about twenty-five years and became the first member of the Virtuosi del Pantheon from the British Isles. Many of his works are to be found in Ireland.

Artists of the twentieth century in Rome include Bernard McDonagh, the Sligo-born painter whose works are to be found in the Irish College and the Ducal palace at Camerino. Breda O'Donoghue-Lucci, the Cork-born artist, has a most impressive portfolio and divides her time between her home in West Cork and Rome. Breda Ennis and Ann Donnelly also work in Rome and carry on an honourable tradition which is by now well established.

Embassy of Ireland to the Holy See

After the ratification of the Lateran Treaty between Italy and the Holy See in 1929, the City of Rome became the capital of two independent sovereign states – Italy and the Vatican City State.

The term Holy See refers to the composite of the authority, jurisdiction and sovereignty vested in and exercised by the Pope and his advisors in the temporal and spiritual direction of the Roman Catholic Church throughout the world. The advisors to the Pope make up the administrative complex of the Holy See, known as the Roman Curia. The Holy See has sovereign jurisdiction over the Vatican City which comprises some 108 acres in the city of Rome. The Holy See is a recognised institution with a legal personality under international law. It can enter into treaties as the juridical equal of a state and can receive diplomatic representatives. The Holy See has formal diplomatic relationships with one hundred and seventy-one states, including all member states of the European Union. Sixty-eight states have resident embassies in Rome accredited to the Holy See.

Ireland established diplomatic relations with the Holy See in 1929. The first Irish Minister, Charles Bewley, took up residence in Rome in the same year. For its part, the Holy See appointed a Nuncio or resident papal representative, Paschal Robinson, in Dublin in 1930.

The Irish Embassy to the Holy See is the official channel for communication between the Irish Government and the Holy See: such communications cover a range of international political, economic, developmental and human rights issues. Over the years, many Irish dignitaries have visited the Holy See. In February 1999, President Mary McAleese made an official visit to Pope John Paul II and senior officials of the Curia. During her visit she said: 'In making the journey to Rome, I am conscious that I am one in a long line of Irish leaders, religious and pilgrims who have followed St Patrick, the Apostle of Ireland, through many centuries up to the present'.

The Embassy maintains contact with the many Irish Roman Catholic religious living and working in Rome. It has contact also with the representatives of other faith communities, Christian and non-Christian, that are in dialogue with the Holy See.

Embassy of Ireland to Italy

The Embassy of Ireland to Italy was established in Rome in 1938. Since then, additional countries have been added to the Irish Ambassador's responsibilities and, besides Italy, now include Libya, Malta and San Marino, to which the Ambassador is accredited on a non-residential basis. The Embassy also provides Ireland's official representation to the Rome-based United Nations organisations – the Food and Agriculture Organization (FAO), the World Food Programme (WFP), the International Fund for Agricultural Development (IFAD) and the International Institute for the Unification of Private Law (UNIDROIT).

The Irish Embassy is the official channel of communication between the Irish Government on the one hand, and the Governments of Italy, Libya, Malta, San Marino and the above-mentioned United Nations organisations on the other. It is the function of the Embassy to conduct and deepen Ireland's bilateral relations with these countries in the political, economic, social and cultural spheres and to participate actively in the policy-making organs of the international organisations.

Another important function of the Embassy is the provision of an efficient passport and consular service to Irish citizens in the Embassy's areas of responsibility and to provide a visa service for foreigners requiring a visa to visit Ireland. Consular services provided by the Embassy include assistance and advice to Irish citizens, particularly in circumstances of distress, for example, lost passports or belongings. Emergency consular problems arising at week-ends can be dealt with by a duty officer if contact is made with the Embassy by telephone (no. 06-6979121).

The Embassy is located at Piazza di Campitelli, 3 (first floor), a short walk from Piazza Venezia, and the public hours from Monday to Friday inclusive are: 10.00-12.30; 15:00-16.30.

The Irish and the United Nations Food and Agricultural Organisation (FAO)

The headquarters of the Food and Agricultural section of the United Nations is located in Rome. Its aim is to assist poor countries in the development of suitable and viable crops and food programmes. It does this on a worldwide basis through sharing scientific expertise and experts in the various areas needing help.

From its inception, the various programmes within the organization have attracted many Irish women and men who have come to Rome or who have gone overseas to promote the aims of this organisation and its programmes. Many of them have served in areas of responsibility and managerial positions.

Irish Pubs in Rome

When you are in Rome you are never very far away from an Irish pub. Go around by the Basilica of St Mary Major and you will find three or four; on the way out to the Basilica of St Paul Outside the Walls, another two or three; next door to the Church of St Paul inside the Walls, downtown close to the Via del Corso, out by the Via Boccea, near Piazza Cavour, over by Largo Argentina. They are all nicely distributed in every part of the city. You would think that an anti-thirst squad had planned it that way!

Irish pubs in the beginning looked as if they wanted to recover the atmosphere of the old-style pubs in Ireland, the all-male-sawdust-on-the-floor variety. Some of the newer ones show more colour and polish, thanks to the designs of their multi-national promoters. Generally speaking you will find them crowded after 22.00. Up to that time you should find plenty of space and a little less smoke. In some places you will find a very welcome happy hour around 21.00 when you will get your pint at half-price.

As for the drink of your choice, if you like draught, you have the choice of Guinness, two varieties of Kilkenny, Harp Lager and Strongbow Cider. If your favourite drink comes in a bottle, your choice is much wider. Romans have taken a very keen interest in beers in recent years. It is obvious that young Italians have changed their taste from the grape to the grain and they like to experiment with different names and countries of origin. If you enjoy a pint of plain, be careful how they pour it. There is a barman by the name of Michael in one of the places over near St Mary Major. It has been said that a pint poured by Michael is a little taste of home.

'Cumann Gealach na Roimhe' – The Irish Club Rome

The Irish Club in Rome was founded in 1993 as a non-profit, non-denominational, non-political Club. It was founded by the active encouragement of the Irish Embassy to provide a cultural focus for Irish people and those interested in Irish Culture in Rome. Through the past years the Club has organised cultural and social events to promote good relations between Ireland and Italy, and as a result boasts several Italian members. The Club has its own constitution and holds an annual general meeting every year in March. The executive committee is elected by the club members during this meeting and a committee member cannot serve for more than two consecutive years.

The activities handled by the club through the past years, besides acting as a citizen's advice bureau, have been céilis, outings, dinners, poetry readings, table quizzes and historical walks. These have all been very well attended as the club has also created that friendly atmosphere of 'home away from home'. The highlight of the social calendar is the Celtic Ball, which is held every year around the St Patrick's Day festivities. Profits from this event are donated to charity and split equally between Italian and Irish charities.

The Club is run by an executive committee made up of four officers and five committee members who take it upon themselves to organise the various events and to provide its members with a regular newsletter. The number of newsletters issued every year is usually five, and each issue covers matters of Irish interest and various events in Rome.

ROME AND THE VATICAN

Vatican City

Following the fall of the Papal States and the growth of the movement for unity in Italy, the relationship between the Catholic Church and the Italian State was peacefully ratified with the signing, by Pope Pius XI and Benito Mussolini, of the Lateran Treaty on 11 February, 1929. Following the Corcordat, the Vatican became an independent, sovereign state, less than half a square kilometre, the smallest state in existence. The Pope is the temporal ruler, a power he delegates to his Secretary of State. The Vatican is surrounded by a wall built by different Popes between 1550 and 1640. As an autonomous state, the Vatican has its own Governor, appointed by the Pope, its own legislature, executive and judiciary. The state also has its own postage-stamps, currency, radio station, newspaper (*L'Osservatore Romano*), security guards, police force and Swiss Guards.

The Basilicas of Rome

The word basilica comes from a Greek word meaning royal house, portico, or House of the King. Essentially, a basilica was a great hall with 'aisles' divided by rows of columns from the central 'nave', which in Christian times usually had a higher ceiling than the rest of the building. At the end of the large centre hall was a rounded area, the apse, where the presiding person sat. In Roman times the basilica was used for both public and private business.

The building of the first Christian basilica is attributed to the Emperor Constantine, ca. 313. Up to this time the celebration of the Eucharist and meetings of Christians usually took place in private houses. He donated the site of the present basilica of St John Lateran to the Pope and began to construct a basilica. Constantine also began the building of the first Basilica of St Peter in Rome, the Basilica of the Nativity in Bethlehem and the Basilica of the Annunciation in Nazareth, among many others. Since that time more than 350 historic churches have been built within Rome's *centro storico*, the historic centre of the city.

Christian Model

The Christians adopted the common model of the basilica for their places of worship with some necessary modifications. In a semicircular apse stood the chair of the presiding bishop and a square altar. The presiding prelate celebrated the Eucharist facing the people, usually towards the east.

The altar was separated from the nave by a low marble divide and there were usually two pulpits for the sacred readings. In some basilicas, a transept extended in front of the sanctuary to facilitate movement and the altar was usually surmounted by a triumphal arch. The wall spaces and the floors were often covered in mosaics and paintings depicting biblical scenes. The entrance was at the opposite end of the nave and outside there was normally a portico and an atrium. This model is still to be seen in the Basilica of St Paul Outside the Walls and in the Basilica of S. Clemente which is under the care of the Irish Dominicans.

Churches with the title of 'Basilica'

A church is called a basilica either by Apostolic permission or immemorial custom. In Rome today there are a number of churches with the title 'basilica' – there are four 'major' basilicas and a number of 'minor' basilicas. The four major basilicas are designated as such because of their 'antiquity, dimensions or fame.' Each of the major basilicas has a 'Holy Door' which is opened at the beginning of each Jubilee Year and closed at the end of the year. They are also called patriarchal because they have been linked with the great churches of early Christendom: St. John Lateran represents the importance of the See of Rome, being the church of the Pope; St Peter's represents the See of Constantinople; St Paul's Outside the Walls, represents the See of Alexandria, and St Mary Major's represents the See of Antioch, where it is believed the Blessed Virgin lived. Wishing to represent the See of Jerusalem, the Church of St Lawrence Outside the Walls was designated as a patriarchal basilica, though not a major one. In order to increase the number of basilicas to seven for the pilgrimage called the 'Roman Basilicas', the Basilicas of The Holy Cross in Jerusalem (Santa Croce) and of St Sebastian, which is in the catacomb of that name, were added to the other five patriarchal basilicas, with the right to grant the appropriate indulgences and blessings. The minor basilicas are thus named when a Pope bestows the title because of their role at various times in the history of the papacy, and with the title go many of the privileges of a major basilica. The Dominican Church of S. Clemente is a minor basilica. Thus, the seven churches where the traditional pilgrim went to pray and gain the Holy Year indulgence are the Basilicas of St Peter, St John Lateran, St Paul Outside the Walls, St Mary Major, St Lawrence Outside the Walls, the Church of the Holy Cross and the Catacombs of St Sebastian, and, for the Jubilee 2000, the Shrine of Our Lady of Divine Love and the Christian Catacombs.

The Catacombs

Contrary to popular belief the catacombs were not secret burial places for Christians. All burial sites were sacred to the Romans. Cemeteries were protected by law but people had to be buried outside the city limits. Jews and Christians were buried, whereas non-Jews and non-Christians burned their dead. In the beginning Christians buried their dead above ground in plots provided by Christian landowners. As numbers increased, the Christians dug into the soft tufa rock, constructed galleries or corridors, and buried their dead in 'loculi' or niches along the galleries. When the Christian religion became the religion of the state in the early fourth century the catacombs were no longer used as burial places but the dead were honoured by various religious celebrations.

The Goths vandalised the tombs in search of treasure and in the eighth and ninth centuries the remaining bones were removed to avoid plundering and commerce in bones. Many of the catacombs were in fact forgotten until rediscovered in 1849.

The catacombs are normally open from 08.30-12.00 and in the afternoons from 15.30 until dusk. The weekly closing day varies with each catacomb.

SECTION II

SUGGESTED ITINERARIES

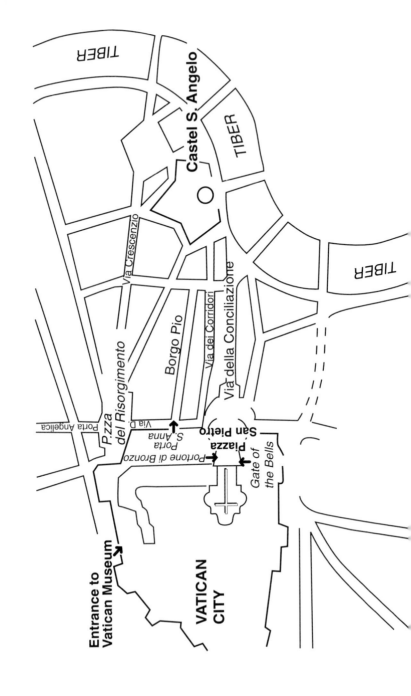

ITINERARY A

THE VATICAN – CASTEL S. ANGELO
*St Peter's Square – Basilica of St Peter – Scavi –
Vatican Museums and Galleries – The Sistine Chapel – Castel S. Angelo*

St Peter's Square and the Basilica of St Peter
Open daily 07.00-19.00 (winter 18.00).

Previous buildings and Present Basilica
An oratory was constructed over the tomb of St Peter in the second century. The Emperor Constantine built a basilica in its place, which was consecrated in 326. In the course of the centuries, the basilica was damaged by the Saracens and suffered further damage from floods and earthquakes. By the middle of the fifteenth century, this construction had become unsafe. In 1505, Pope Julius II entrusted Donato Bramante with the task of replacing it. His design was for a church in the form of a Greek cross with four arms of equal length extending from a central area around the high altar. Bramante was succeeded in 1514 by Raphael, Peruzzi, Sangallo and Michelangelo. The latter worked on the basilica from 1546 until his death at the age of 89 in 1564. Inspired by the cathedral of Florence and the Pantheon, Michelangelo designed the dome, which was completed by Giacomo della Porta in 1588-1589. It is an architectural masterpiece, which soars above the tomb of St Peter.

Pope Paul V decided to change the design to that of a Latin cross – the upright is longer than the cross beam – and the front nave was extended by the architect Carlo Maderna to cover the area that had been occupied by Constantine's basilica. The funerary monuments from this basilica were transferred to the Grottoes which had been built in 1575-1605 under the new basilica. Bernini succeeded Maderna and worked on the basilica for fifty years. He was responsible for much of the decoration of the interior. The basilica was consecrated in 1626, the 1,300th anniversary of the consecration of the basilica of Constantine. With an area of 15,000 square metres, the new basilica of St Peter is a majestic building which incorporates masterpieces by the greatest artists of the seventeenth century.

St Peter's Square
Bernini began the construction of the Piazza with its famous colonnade in 1656. The Piazza, in fact, is more elliptical than square. There are 284 four-deep columns of travertine crowned with a roof adorned with a fine cornice along which are arranged 140 statues of saints sculpted by the pupils at the school of Bernini.

The Obelisk
The obelisk, which had been brought by the Emperor Caligula from Heliopolis in 37 AD and had once stood in the Circus of Nero, was transferred by Pope Sixtus V in 1582 to its present position in the square between two large fountains.

Portico and the Holy Door
The design of the flooring is by Bernini and the equestrian statue of Constantine, on the right, is also by him. The statue on the left, of Charlemagne on horseback, is by Agostino Cornacchini. Over the central entrance to the portico is the much restored mosaic by Giotto of Christ walking on the water, which was originally in the old basilica. The central door of the basilica dates from the fifteenth century and also comes from the previous structure. The farthest door to the right is the Holy Door (Porta Santa),which is opened at the beginning of a Jubilee Year and closed at the end of the year. The Holy Father will open this door on 24 December 1999, during the Christmas Vigil Mass, to inaugurate the Jubilee Year 2000. On the Feast of the Epiphany, 6 January 2001, the Great Jubilee Year will officially be brought to an end with the closing of the Holy Door by the Pope.

Inside the Basilica
Inside the basilica, in front of the central door, there is a round porphyry slab where Charlemagne and his successors as Holy Roman Emperors knelt to be crowned by the Pope. In the first chapel in the aisle on the right is the famous masterpiece, the Vatican *Pietà,* sculpted by Michelangelo when he was twenty-five years of age: it is the only work which bears the sculptor's name. The statue was attacked by a deranged man in 1972 and it has since been protected by a glass partition. Farther

down on the right of the nave is the thirteenth century black statue of St Peter in bronze – now considered to be the work of di Cambio (ca. 1296) – whose foot is gradually being worn away by the people as they touch it.

Chapel of the Blessed Sacrament
Bernini's ciborium of 1674 on the altar of the Chapel of the Blessed Sacrament is modelled on the temple of Bramante at the Church of S. Pietro in Montorio (see p. 120). Behind the altar is Pietro da Cortona's *Trinity*, a rare example of a painting in the basilica. Other chapels are adorned by mosaic copies of famous paintings, including Raphael's *Transfiguration*.

Papal Altar and Baldacchino
The interior of the basilica is dominated by the twenty-nine-metre high bronze Baroque baldacchino (canopy) over the Papal altar. This was built by Bernini in the period 1624-1633 and inaugurated by the Barberini Pope, Urban VIII. The bronze from which it was made is said to have been taken from the Pantheon.

SCAVI
The Tomb of St Peter
Christians on pilgrimage come to the Basilica of St Peter to renew their faith at the tomb of the Apostle who was the first Vicar of Christ. St Peter was crucified upside down in the nearby Circus of Nero in 64 and buried in a necropolis nearby. Excavations (*scavi*) conducted over the period 1940-1964 confirmed that this necropolis was situated under the present basilica, the left side of which overlaps the site of the Circus of Nero. One can apply in writing or in person to visit the excavations to the *Ufficio Scavi* (Tel. 06-6988-5318; Fax 06-6988-5518), which is approached through the passageway under the Arch of the Bells, at the top left-hand corner of St Peter's Square.

Scriptural reflections during visit to the Basilica of St Peter:
As Jesus passed along the Sea of Galilee, he saw Simon and his brother Andrew casting a net into the sea – for they were fishermen. And Jesus said to them, 'Follow me and I will make you fishers for people.' And immediately they left their nets and followed him. (Mark 1: 16-18)

And he went up the mountain and called to him those whom he wanted and they came to him. And he appointed twelve, whom he also named apostles, to be with him, and to be sent out to proclaim the message, and to have authority to cast out demons. So he appointed the twelve: Simon, to whom he gave the name Peter... (Mark 3: 1.3-16)

He said to them, 'But who do you say that I am?' Simon Peter answered, 'You are the Messiah, the Son of the living God.' And Jesus answered him, 'Blessed are you, Simon son of Jonah! For flesh and blood has not revealed this to you, but my Father in heaven. And I tell you, you are Peter, and on this rock I will build my church, and the gates of Hades will not prevail against it. I will give you the keys of the kingdom of heaven, and whatever you bind on earth will be bound in heaven, and whatever you loose on earth will be loosed in heaven.' (Mt 16: 13-19)

The Crypt (Grottoes). Weekdays 08.00-17.00

After you enter St Peter's Basilica, once you have seen the *Pietà,* walk towards the main altar. In the nave on your right hand side you will see the black statue of St Peter and beyond that a statue of St Longinus holding a spear in one of the great pillars supporting the dome. Beneath the statue you should find a sign which indicates that you should go down the steps to visit the tombs of the Popes including many of the recent Popes – Pius XII, John XXIII, Paul VI and John Paul I. On your way to the tombs you will pass a number of small chapels. The third chapel on the right is the Irish Chapel which is dedicated to Saint Columbanus, also known as Columban, who represents all Irish missionaries.

The Irish Chapel, dedicated to St Columban / The Crypt

St Columban (ca. 543-615), who represents all Irish missionaries, was born in Leinster. After attending the school of St Sinnell on Cleenish Island in Lough Erne, he became a monk in the monastery of Bangor. After his priestly ordination he taught in the monastery for a number of years. Desiring 'to go on pilgrimage for Christ,' and 'to be an exile for Christ,' he set sail with twelve companions for Burgundy in 570. He established monasteries at Annegray, Luxeuil and Fontaines, which were based on the prevailing severe Irish monastic rule and observance. Luxeuil became a great centre of learning and the model for many monasteries throughout Europe. Columban was expelled from Luxeuil in 610 because he denounced king Theuderic. Having passed through Switzerland, where he founded a monastery at Bregenz, he crossed the Alps about 613 and established his last foundation at Bobbio in Northern Italy, where he died in 615 in a cave while praying. Columban greatly influenced the spirit and culture of Europe and he left a very valuable corpus of spiritual works. These works show why he was renowned for both his sanctity and his learning. There are many places named after him in the areas where he travelled that bear testimony to his influence and spirit. In the words of the late Cardinal Tomás O'Fiaich, the

European Irish person of the twentieth century 'may find inspiration and courage in the words of this sixth century pioneer, Southern-born, Northern-trained, Irish-speaking, European-minded, who set his country on a new path to which it is now returning fourteen centuries later'.

The idea of having an Irish Chapel dedicated to St Columban in the Crypt of St Peter's Basilica was conceived and promoted by Mr Patrick J. Walshe, Ambassador of Ireland to the Holy See, 1946-1954. At that time, extensive excavations were being carried out around the Tomb of St Peter. The project was approved by Pope Pius XII on the Feastday of St Columban and the Ambassador was officially informed of the decision by Monsignor Montini, later to become Pope Paul VI, with the following telegram of 23 November 1949:

> His Holiness has learned with much gratification of the project of erecting a Chapel to St Columban in the Crypt of the Vatican Basilica. Taking the occasion of the Feastday of this great Irish Missionary, the Holy Father voices the fervent hope that with the ready cooperation of the Irish Nation this praiseworthy plan may soon be realized. As an earnest sign of his paternal interest the Supreme Pontiff imparts to Your Excellency and to all those who promote and further this blessed undertaking His special Apostolic Blessing.

The estimated cost of the project was £12,000 and the necessary funds were kindly provided by the Irish Branch of the Knights of St Columbanus. Contributions were made by some Irish Bishops, particularly the Archbishops of Armagh, Dublin and Tuam, and by prominent Irish lay people. Technical difficulties delayed the realisation of the project and an altar was erected in the Crypt of St Peter's in honour of St Columban while work continued on the Chapel. Bishop Vincent Hanly of Elphin celebrated the first Mass in honour of St Columban at the altar on the Saint's Feastday, 23 November, during the Holy Year 1950.

The Chapel was not completed until the second half of 1954 and it was finally dedicated on 11 September 1954, with a Mass celebrated by the then Archbishop of Dublin, John Charles McQuaid. The Ambassador, after so much effort, was not able to attend the dedication ceremony due to illness. The Ambassador completed his term in Rome within a few weeks of the dedication.

Apart from the mosaic behind the altar, the completed Chapel lacked other decorations for some time. Over the course of the following years, donations for its completion were received, all items having a celtic design. Messrs Gunning & Son, Ltd., Dublin, donated the six silver candlesticks and the crucifix; the Mass Charts were donated by the Irish Post Office Engineering and Workers Unions, and the Dunemer carpet for the predella in front of the altar was the gift of Dr Brendan Senior, Dublin. Recently the Chapel has been refurnished. The altar has been brought forward and the mosaic depicting St Columban and his followers, *Peregrinantes pro Christo* (*Pilgrims for Christ*), with the images of Bangor and Bobbio at the sides, has been completed. Once again the Irish Branch of the Knights of St Columbanus has generously provided the necessary funds. His Grace, Most Reverend Séan Brady, Archbishop of Armagh and Primate of All Ireland, dedicated the renovated Chapel on 22 June 1999. The Irish Bishops, on an *ad limina* visit to Rome, concelebrated the Eucharist with the Archbishop.

The Chapel has been visited by many Irish politicians and distinguished people, including President Eamon de Valera and President Patrick Hilary. On Easter Monday, 11 April 1966, representatives of the Irish community in Rome attended a Mass in memory of the Irish Leaders who forfeited their lives in the Easter Rising of 1916. The Mass was celebrated by Cardinal Michael Browne OP, and the poem 'Easter 1916' by W.B. Yeats was included in the prayer service:

> We know their dream; enough
> To know they dreamed and are dead;
> And what if excess of love
> Bewildered them till they died?
> I write it out in a verse –
> MacDonagh and MacBride
> And Connolly and Pearse
> Now and in time to be,
> Wherever green is worn
> Are changed, changed utterly:
> A terrible beauty was born.

The Roof and Dome

The entrance to the dome is marked *Cupola*. You ascend to the roof by lift or by a stair. The view of the square, the Via della Conciliazione and the surrounding skyline is worthwhile. From the roof, two stairways lead to the interior gallery of the dome which gives a breathtaking view of the interior of the basilica – the altar, the mosaics and the floor which is fifty metres below. You begin to realise the immensity, the size, the symmetry and the beauty of the building.

A narrow and curving stairway between the two domes leads upward to a viewing deck under the Lantern. The deck is 537 steps from ground level. From here there is a wonderful view of the Vatican, the city of Rome and, on a fine day, there is a view of the Alban Hills.

VATICAN MUSEUM
Viale Vaticano.
Summer: Monday-Friday 08.45-17.00;
Winter and Saturday 08.45-13.45. Entry up to one hour before closing time. Closed Sundays, except last Sunday of month, when admission is free. The museum is a ten-minute walk from the right side of the square, facing St Peter's. At the entrance to the museum there are lifts and stairs to the ticket office where a ticket costs ITL 18.000. Nearby is a post office, a writing room, a book shop and a money exchange office. Having passed the ticket check-point, recorded cassette guides are available (you need to leave an official document when renting). You then enter an open courtyard, with the entrance to the picture gallery (*Pinacoteca*) on the right and the entrance to the museum on the left. Near the entrance to the picture gallery, stairs lead down to a restaurant and toilets and to a patio with a very good view of the gardens and the basilica.

The Picture Gallery
The picture gallery (*Pinacoteca*) contains paintings and tapestries from the eleventh to the nineteenth centuries, including some which Napoleon had removed to Paris. Notable pictures are: *Transfiguration* by Raphael, *St Jerome* by Leonardo da Vinci, *Pietà* by Giovanni Bellini, *Madonna and Child* by Fra Angelico, *Peter's Denial* and the *Deposition* by Caravaggio, *Crucifixion of St Peter* by Guido Reni.

The Vatican Galleries
There are over seven kilometres of galleries in the Vatican Palace or museum. There are four suggested tours – A, B, C, and D. Tour A takes about 90 minutes and includes the Sistine Chapel. Tour D takes up to five hours. The Sistine Chapel is approached by passing through many halls and galleries where works of sculpture (Gallery of the Candelabra), tapestries designed by pupils of Raphael, maps, mosaics, paintings and precious manuscripts and books are on display (Room of the Immaculate Conception). The longer tours include Raphael's Stanze and the Chapel of Nicholas V which was painted by Fra Angelico.

The Vatican Library

The Vatican Library collection began in 1447 with 340 books belonging to Pope Nicholas V. It now houses thousands of famous and irreplaceable manuscripts, codices and books, including the Sala Sistina and works from the fourth and later centuries, which include early copies of Virgil, poems in Michelangelo's handwriting, and letters written by Henry VIII to Anne Boleyn.

The archives also include a letter written in ink, on a page of a copy book, by the Venerable Matt Talbot (1856-1925), a year before he died, to the Superior of St Columban's, Navan:

> Matt Talbot have done no work for past 18 months. I have been sick and given over by Priest and Doctor. I don't think I will work any more. There one pound from me and ten shillings from my sister.

The letter was presented to Pope Paul VI in 1977 on the occasion of his eightieth birthday by the Very Rev. Father Morgan Costello, the Vice Postulator of the cause, and the Superior and Community of St Columban's, Navan.

THE SISTINE CHAPEL

The Sistine Chapel is named after its builder, Pope Sixtus IV (1471-1484). It was intended as the chapel for the Papal Palaces and its dimensions are said to be those of the temple of Solomon in Jerusalem. It was completed in 1481 and in the following two years was decorated by the foremost artists of the time, Perugino, Signorelli, Botticelli and Ghirlandaio. Paintings on the wall to the right of the altar represent scenes from the life of Moses, and those on the opposite wall are parallel scenes from the life of Christ. Above these are portraits of the early Popes by the same artists.

In 1508, Pope Julius II (1503-1513) commissioned Michelangelo, then thirty-three years of age, to paint the ceiling. Michelangelo refused on the grounds that he was a sculptor and not a painter, but the Pope insisted. Working with little assistance, Michelangelo completed the commission in four years. In 1534, Pope Paul III commissioned Michelangelo, then sixty-six years of age, to paint the *Last Judgement* above the main altar. Michelangelo completed the task in 1541. Michelangelo's work in the Sistine Chapel is one of the world's greatest artistic achievements.

The Ceiling

The ceiling, which has recently been cleaned and restored to its original beauty and colour – a task that took ten years – tells the story of the creation of the universe, the planets, the animals, the human race, humankind's fall from grace, the deluge and the salvation of Noah with his subsequent drinking spree. These scenes are surrounded by frescoes of the classical Sybils and the great Prophets of the Old Testament. Michelangelo's work on the ceiling is imbued with the vitality and exuberance of the spirit of the Renaissance, and his figures reflect the approximation of the human to the Divine and the consequent diminution of that divine image in humankind caused by the rupture of sin.

Last Judgement

In the great fresco of the *Last Judgement,* painted in 1541, the artist is much more subdued. This fresco, which has also been restored, reflects recent events in Rome at the time, such as the divisions caused by the Reformation and the counter Reformation and the sacking of Rome in 1527, events which brought confusion and caused dismay. The Christ of the *Last Judgement* is a sombre and somewhat frightening Judge, while Mary seems to shrink from the scene of the damned who are cast into hell in a descending movement on the right side of the fresco. Those called to eternal life are depicted rising in an upward movement on the left side of the fresco. Underneath the figure of Christ is the figure of St Bartholomew with his flayed skin on which can be seen a self-portrait of Michelangelo.

CASTEL S. ANGELO – HADRIAN'S TOMB

Lungotevere Castello.
Weekdays 09.00-21.00. Entry up to one hour before closing time.
Leaving the Vatican by Via della Conciliazione, you arrive at Castel S. Angelo. The building gets its name from the legend which relates the vision of Pope Gregory the Great in 590, in which he saw an angel putting his sword back in its scabbard to signify the end of a devastating plague. The Emperor Hadrian began the structure of the original building which he intended as his burial place. Succeeding emperors of the second century were buried in the building, which later became a fortress at the time of the barbarian invasions. Since the twelfth century the building has been under papal control and, by turns, has been a prison and a place of refuge for Popes in times of invasions. A covered passage connecting the Castel with the Vatican was constructed in the fifteenth century by Alexander VI. Castel S. Angelo is now a museum with four floors open to visitors. They include the Papal Apartments, some interesting frescoes and a collection of armour. There is also a superb view of the Tiber.

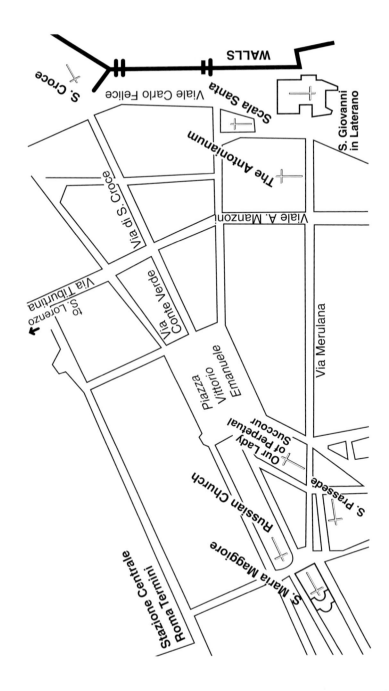

ITINERARY B

BASILICA OF ST MARY MAJOR
BASILICA OF ST JOHN LATERAN
*Basilica of St Mary Major – Church of SS. Prassede and Pudenziana –
Russian Church – Church of St Alphonsus (Shrine of Our Lady of
Perpetual Help) – Basilica of St John Lateran –
Basilica of the Holy Cross in Jerusalem –
Basilica of St Lawrence Outside the Walls*

S. MARIA MAGGIORE – BASILICA OF ST MARY MAJOR
Piazza S. Maria Maggiore.
07.00-20.00/Winter 19.00
Short walk from Termini Station.
The name of the first church built on the site was St Mary's of the Snows,
commemorating the legend of its origin. On the night of 4-5 August 352,
the Virgin appeared in a vision to a rich Roman named John, telling him
to build a church in her honour on a site where he would find snow the
following morning. On the same night, the Virgin also appeared to Pope
Liberius (352-366), and told him to go to the top of the Esquiline Hill
where he would find snow and where a great church should be built.
Pope Liberius and John met in the morning and the Pope traced the
outline of a church in the snow. John built the church of St Mary's of the
Snow whose feast is celebrated annually on 5 August. The present
building was built by Pope Sixtus III (432-440). After the Council of
Ephesus in 431, the church was enlarged in honour of the doctrine that
Mary was truly the Mother of Jesus, the Son of God made man.

Inside the basilica, the paving is classic cosmatesque work of the
twelfth century and the magnificent ceiling is said to be gilded with some
of the first gold brought back from the New World and presented to

Alexander VI by Ferdinand and Isabella of Spain. Between the ceiling and the marble columns are mosaics depicting, on the left, biblical scenes from the lives of Abraham, Isaac and Jacob, and over the arch, scenes from the life of Christ. On the right are other Old Testament scenes featuring Moses and Joshua.

The high altar contains relics of St Matthew, among others. In the confessio (crypt) below are relics of the true crib, and relics of St Jerome who spent many years in Bethlehem translating the Bible into Latin. The tomb of the Bernini family is also here. The Torriti thirteenth century mosaics of the apse celebrate the doctrine of the Council of Ephesus that Mary is the Mother of God. Beneath these is the large mosaic, also by Torriti, of the Dormition of the Virgin. The Borghese Chapel (Lady Chapel), which is the the last chapel on the left, contains papal tombs and the twelfth century picture of a Madonna and Child, framed in agate. Opposite is the ornate Sistina Chapel of Domenico Fontana with the tombs of Pius V and Sixtus V.

Scriptural reflection during visit to the Basilica of St Mary Major:
In the sixth month the angel Gabriel was sent by God to a town in Galilee called Nazareth, to a virgin engaged to a man whose name was Joseph, of the house of David. The virgin's name was Mary. And he came to her and said, 'Greetings, favoured one! The Lord is with you.' But she was much perplexed by his words and pondered what sort of greeting this might be. The angel said to her, Do not be afraid, Mary, for you have found favour with God. And now you will conceive in your womb and bear a son, and you will name him Jesus. He will be great, and will be called Son of the Most High, and the Lord God will give to him the throne of his ancestor David. He will reign over the house of Jacob forever, and of his kingdom there will be no end.' Mary said to the angel, 'How can this be, since I am a virgin?' The angel said to her, 'The Holy Spirit will come upon you, and the power of the Most High will overshadow you: therefore the child to be born will be holy; he will be called Son of God. And now, your relative Elizabeth in her old age has also conceived a son; and this is the sixth month for her who was said to be barren. For nothing will be impossible with God.; Then Mary said, 'Here I am, the servant of the Lord; let it be with me according to your word.' ... In those days Mary set out and went with haste to a Judean town in the hill country, where she entered the house of Zechariah and greeted Elizabeth. When Elizabeth heard Mary's greeting the child leaped in her womb. And Elizabeth was filled with the Holy Spirit and exclaimed with a loud cry, 'Blessed are you among women, and

blessed is the fruit of your womb. And why has this happened to me, that the mother of my Lord comes to me? For as soon as I heard the sound of your greeting, the child in my womb leaped for joy. And blessed is she who believed that there would be a fulfilment of what was spoken to her by the Lord.
And Mary said,

'My soul magnifies the Lord,
and my spirit rejoices in God
my Saviour,
for he has looked with favour on
the lowliness of his servant.
Surely, from now on all
generations will call me blessed;
For the Mighty One has done
great things for me,
and holy is his name.
His mercy is for those who fear him
from generation to generation.
He has shown strength with his arm;
he has scattered the proud in
the thoughts of their hearts.
He has brought down the powerful from their thrones,
and lifted up the lowly;
he has filled the hungry with good things,
and sent the rich away empty.
He has helped his servant Israel,
in remembrance of his mercy,
according to the promise he made to our ancestors,
to Abraham and to his descendants forever.' (Lk 1: 26-56)

S. PRASSEDE – S. PRAXEDES
Via S. Prassede
(off Via Merulana, on the right, on leaving St Mary Major).
S. PUDENZIANA, Via Urbana.
A church stood on this site in the early fifth century, built on what was traditionally believed to be a house that served as a meeting place for early Christians. The present building, much restored, was completed in the ninth century. It is dedicated to St Praxedes, sister of St Pudenziana, whose church is on Via Urbana. The saints are said to be daughters of Pudens, the Roman Senator, who is mentioned in the Second letter of St Paul to Timothy, Chapter 2:21, 'Do your best to come before winter.

Eubulus sends greetings to you, as do Pudens and Linus and Claudia and all the brothers and sisters.' Tradition has it that Pudens was host to both St Peter and St Paul in his house. It was thought at one time that it was on the site of this house that the Church of St Pudenziana was built. In the Church of St Praxedes there are famous mosaics in the apse and on the arches in front of it. In the crypt under the altar are the relics of the two sister saints. On the right side of the church is the Byzantine Chapel of St Zeno with ninth-century mosaics. Pope Paschal built this chapel in honour of his mother whose portrait, in mosaic, is to be found in the chapel. In a section on the right is a marble fragment said to be part of the pillar at which Christ was scourged.

In the Church of St Pudenziana, on the apse, is the pre-Byzantine mosaic of Christ with the Apostles Peter and Paul and two women, thought by some to be Sts Pudenziana and Praxedes.

RUSSIAN CHURCH
Via Carlo Alberto (on the left on leaving the Basilica of St Mary Major). Approached by steps on Via Carlo Alberto is the Catholic Church of the Byzantine Rite. The church is known as the 'Russian Church', as it is attached to the Institute of Oriental Studies and the Russicum, or Russian College. The present church is generally of the Baroque tradition of the eighteenth century, and its icons and sanctuary are very beautiful. Visitors usually find the Sunday Liturgy very interesting.

SHRINE OF OUR LADY OF PERPETUAL HELP
Via Merulana 27.
07.00-19.30.
Metro A, Station Vittorio Emanuele; Metro B, Station Cavour.
Buses from Termini Station, 16, 714.
Near the Basilica of St Mary Major, on the Via Merulana, stands the Redemptorist gothic Church of St Alphonsus de Liguori, which was built in 1855-1859. The original icon of Our Lady of Perpetual Help, whose devotees include many Irish people, is over the main altar. It was brought to Rome from the Island of Crete in the fifteenth century and for over three centuries was the centre of devotion in the Church of St Matthew on the Esquiline hill. When this church was destroyed by Napoleon's troops, the Augustinians brought the icon to the Church of St Mary in Posterula where it remained until 1866. In that year, Pope Pius IX entrusted the icon to the Redemptorists and asked them to spread devotion to Mary under the title of 'Our Lady of Perpetual Help'. The Perpetual Novena, which began in St Louis in the United States of America in 1927, has made a notable contribution to the spread of this

devotion. The Novena is celebrated in English at the Shrine each Tuesday at 17.00.

S. GIOVANNI IN LATERANO – BASILICA OF ST JOHN LATERAN
Piazza S. Giovanni in Laterano, Metro A, Station S Giovanni.
07.00-19.00; Winter 18.00.
At the end of the Via Merulana is the first of the Roman basilicas, founded by Constantine I ca. 314-318, and dedicated to Christ the Redeemer. It was built on land that was originally owned by the family of Plautius Lateranus, a patrician put to death by Nero. Later additions to the title include St John the Baptist and St John the Apostle. The basilica is the cathedral of the diocese of Rome and an inscription describes it as 'Mother and Head of all Churches in Rome and in the World'. Until 1870, St. John Lateran was the place where the Popes were crowned and it was the site of five General Councils of the Church, the first held in 1123. Pope Boniface VIII announced the celebration of the first Holy Year in St John Lateran in 1300.

The present building dates from the seventeenth century when Pope Innocent X commissioned Borromini to rebuild the basilica: a number of previous buildings had been fully or partly destroyed over the centuries by the Vandals, by an earthquake and by numerous fires. The façade dates from the eighteenth century and it is surmounted by giant statues of Christ, John the Baptist, John the Apostle, and Doctors of the Church.

Interior
In the interior of the church there are huge early eighteenth century Baroque statues of the Apostles in the niches of the pillars. The papal altar contains many relics, among which are said to be the heads of St Peter and St Paul and the wooden altar used by St Peter. There are many fragments and copies of mosaics belonging to buildings that were destroyed or damaged. A door in the left aisle gives entry to the cloisters (Weekdays 09.00-12.30 and 15.00-18.00; Winter 17.00).

The Piazza and Obelisk
In the Piazza of S. Giovanni is the largest extant Egyptian obelisk and the oldest in the city. It is approximately thirty-one metres high, excluding the support, and dates back to the city of Thebes in the fifteenth century BC. It was rediscovered in the Circus Maximus in three pieces in 1587.

The Baptistery
The famous octagonal Baptistery of St John, built by Constantine at the

beginning of the fourth century, is also found in the Piazza. Today the original 'singing' doors – so called because they make a 'singing' sound when opened – are preserved in the Chapel of St John the Baptist. In the Chapel of Sts Cyprian and Justina (or Sts Secunda and Rufina) is the famous mosaic of the vine, which dates from the fifth century.

The Palace
The Lateran Palace, which was originally founded by Constantine, was the home of the Popes from the fourth century until the exile in Avignon, 1309-1377, after which the Popes took up residence in the Vatican. The palace was completely restored in the sixteenth century for use as the summer residence of the Pope. However, the Quirinal Palace was chosen instead. One part of the old Lateran Palace which survived is on the opposite side of the road and houses the Scala Santa, the Holy Stairs, which are now covered in wood. According to tradition, these are the steps from the stairways in Pilate's house on which Jesus walked after he had been condemned.

S. CROCE IN GERUSALEMME – BASILICA OF THE HOLY CROSS IN JERUSALEM
Piazza Santa Croce.
One of the traditional seven pilgrim churches, the church was founded sometime after 326, according to tradition, by St Helena, mother of the Emperor Constantine, being built within the confines of the Imperial Palace. It was to be a shrine for a fragment of the true Cross brought from Jerusalem by Helena. The church was rebuilt in the early twelfth century and renovated in the eighteenth century. In the lower chapel are remains of some of the twelfth century mosaics and in the Chapel of the Relics are preserved the piece of the true Cross and other relics of the Passion.

Scriptural reflections during visit to the Basilica of the Holy Cross:

Jesus said to them: 'The Son of Man must undergo great sufferings, and be rejected by the elders, chief priests, and scribes, and be killed, and on the third day be raised.' Then he said to them all, 'If any want to become my followers, let them deny themselves and take up their cross daily and follow me'. (Lk 9:21-23)

Pilate then called together the chief priests, the leaders, and the people, and said to them, 'You brought me this man as one who was perverting the people; and here I have examined him in your presence and have not found this man guilty of any of your charges against him. Neither has Herod, for he sent him back to us. Indeed, he has done nothing to deserve death. I will therefore have him flogged and release him.' Then they all shouted out together, 'Away with this fellow! Release Barabbas for us!' (This was a man who had been put in prison for an insurrection that had taken place in the city, and for murder.) Pilate, wanting to release Jesus, addressed them again; but they kept shouting, 'Crucify, crucify him!' A third time he said to them, Why, what evil has he done? I have found in him no ground for the sentence of death; I will therefore have him flogged and then release him.'

But they kept urgently demanding that he should be crucified; and their voices prevailed. So Pilate gave his verdict that their demands should be granted... When they came to the place that is called the Skull, they crucified Jesus there with the criminals. (Lk 23:13-49)

S. LORENZO FUORI DALLE MURA – BASILICA OF ST LAWRENCE OUTSIDE THE WALLS
Via Tiburtina, Bus 71 from Piazza S. Silvestro; Bus 11 from Colosseum. 06.30-12.00; 15.30-18.30.
One of the traditional seven churches of pilgrimage, it honours the martyr of the third century who was roasted alive. The Emperor Constantine built the original church which is now approached by stairs leading down from the more recent church. In the lower church is the catacomb where St Lawrence is buried. Also to be found here is the tomb of Pope Pius IX, who died in 1878. The basilica was damaged by bombs during the Second World War and has now been restored. Near the basilica is the entrance to the huge cemetery called the Campo Verano, where a number of Irish Institutes and Communities have their own burial crypts.

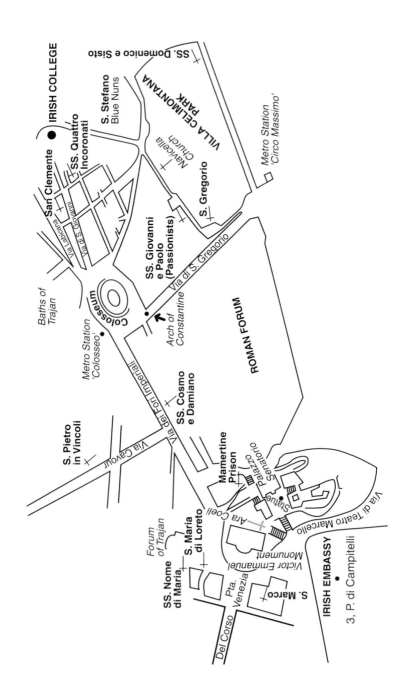

ITINERARY C

THE CAPITOL – THE COLOSSEUM – IRISH COLLEGE
The Capitol – The Forum – Mamertine Prison –
Church of SS. Cosmos and Damian – The Colosseum –
Church of St Peter in Chains – Basilica of St Clement –
Church of St Stephen – Pontifical Irish College

CAMPIDOGLIO - CAPITOLINE HILL, Piazza del Campidoglio.
CAPITOLINE MUSEUM AND PALACE OF THE CONSERVATORI
09.00-19.00. Sun 09.00-18.45. Closed Mon.

Separated from the busy Piazza Venezia by the huge Victor Emmanuel II monument, completed in 1911 to celebrate the unity of Italy, is the Capitoline Hill. It was the most famous of the seven hills of Rome and was the centre of the old Roman world, with its Temple of Jupiter Capitolinus where the Senate met each year and the Temple of Juno Moneta – on the site of a Roman mint: whence the English word 'money' – now the Church of Santa Maria d'Aracoeli. The name of the church comes from the altar placed on the site by the Emperor Augustus because of the oracle of the Sibyl which was thought to refer to the coming of Christ. The name 'Ara Coeli', the residence of the Archbishop of Armagh, comes from this church. The church has the famous crib and statue of the Infant Jesus, the *Bambino*, much loved and venerated by the people of Rome. (The present infant replaces one stolen some years ago).

The original equestrian bronze statue of Marcus Aurelius, designed by Michelangelo, which once stood in the centre of the Piazza, is now in the Capitoline Musem, which is on the left side of the piazza when facing the statue. It has been replaced in the piazza by a copy. In the Capitoline Museum, on the right, are many famous works of art that have been preserved from the past, such as the *Marble Faun*, the *Capitoline Venus*, the *Dying Gaul.* In the Palace of the Conservatori is the sixth-century BC bronze *Capitoline Wolf,* the painting of *Romulus and Remus Suckled by the She Wolf* by Rubens, and the bronze statue of the *Spinarius (Boy with the Thorn).*

From the side of the of the Palazzo Senatorio, the building between the museums, you can look over the Forum and see the Arch of Septimius Severus on the left, on the right are the three columns of the Temple of Castor and Pollux and in the centre the three remaining columns of the Temple of Vespasian.

THE FORUM
Via dei Fori Imperiali.
Entrances at Largo Romolo e Remo 5-6 and Piazza S. Maria Nova (near Arch of Titus).
Sundays and Holidays 10.00-14.00
On the left, between the Capitoline Hill and the Colosseum, the Via dei Fori Imperiali divides the Roman Forum (09.00-1 hour before sunset). On the right of the Via dei Fori are the forums of the cultural and political centre of life during the Republic – and the Imperial Fora. On the left hand side of the Via dei Fori are those built by succeeding emperors, of which the most impressive remains are the Trajan Markets (October/March 09.00-13.30; April/September 09.00-18.00: Closed Mondays) and Trajan's Column with its interior spiral stairway. The column, almost thirty metres high, was completed in four years; the frieze has 2,500 figures celebrating the Emperor's defeat of the Dacians, in what is now modern Romania. The statue of Trajan which stood at the top of the column was replaced by one of St Peter in 1588.

MAMERTINE PRISON
Via del Tulliano.
09.00-12.00; 14.30-17.00.
Walking from the Capitoline Hill towards the Colosseum, Via del Tulliano on the right leads to the Church of S. Pietro in Carcere built on the site of a water system, probably dating from the invasion of the Gauls in 390 BC. It was later used as a prison for the enemies of Rome and many vanquished leaders died there, either of starvation or they were strangled, the only entrance to the cistern being the hole in the floor through which those to be starved to death were thrown.

Tradition has it that St Peter was imprisoned here by Nero. The prison is now a chapel beneath the Church of S. Giuseppe dei Falegnami (Church of St Joseph, Patron of Carpenters) and stairs leading down to the prison. There is a relief showing St Peter baptising his jailers.

SS. Cosmo e Damiano – Church of Saints Cosmo and Damian
Via dei Fori Imperiali

Continuing towards the Colosseum, on the right, is the church built in honour of the two martyred brothers, Cosmos and Damian. Officials of the Emperor Constantine I, the brothers were executed by his successor. The present eighteenth-century building retains the famous mosaic of Christ seated in glory and the Apostles, Saints Peter and Paul, and Saints Cosmos and Damian. In the cloisters is a very large and famous crib from Naples dating from the seventeenth century.

The Colosseum
Piazza del Colosseo, Metro B, Station Colosseo.
09.00-16.00. Summer: 19.00; Sunday and Wednesday 09.00-13.00.

The present ruins are a pale image of the magnificent marble-faced stadium erected on marshy ground, originally with a circumference of about a third of a mile. The building was begun by the Emperor Vespasian and finished by his son, Titus, in 80 AD. The arena could accommodate more than 50,000 spectators. In the event of too much rain or sun, an awning could be spread over the top of the arena. The opening ceremony lasted for three months and the programme featured fights between wild animals and combats between pairs or groups of gladiators. In the arena it is possible to see the remains of the underground passages and storage places where the animals and slaves were kept. Some Christians suffered martyrdom here. The building was abandoned and plundered for many centuries until it was declared a sacred place in the eighteenth century. On the right of the entrance to the Colosseum stands the triumphal arch commemorating the victories of Constantine. The Pope usually leads the Way of the Cross in the Colosseum on the evening of Good Friday.

S. Pietro in Vincoli – Church of St Peter in Chains
Piazza di S. Pietro in Vincoli (off Via Cavour), Metro B, Station Cavour.
07.00-12.30; 15.30-18.00.

It is thought that Pope Sixtus III (432-440) built this church in 432 – the year St Patrick returned to Ireland to preach the Gospel. A glass case under the High Altar contains two sets of chains: one is said to be the chains which bound St Peter when imprisoned in Jerusalem; the other set is that which enchained him during his stay in the nearby Mamertine prison. Legend has it that the two sets immediately interlinked when they were brought together for the first time.

In the right transept is the magnificent figure of Michelangelo's *Moses*, the prophet who received from God on Mount Sinai the tablets with the

Ten Commandments. The figure was meant to be one of forty sculptures for the tomb of Julius II planned for St Peter's. The figures of Leah and Rachel, on either side of Moses, are also by Michelangelo, and represent the active and contemplative life.

S. CLEMENTE – BASILICA OF ST CLEMENT
Via di S. Giovanni in Laterano, 108, Metro B, Station Colosseo
09.00-12.00 [except Sun]; 15.30-18.00.
This well-preserved basilica, which has been in the possession of the Irish Dominicans since 1677, is thought to be dedicated to the fourth pope, St Clement (97-98). The site actually consists of three superimposed churches. Underneath the present church is a shrine of Mithras with a sacrificial altar and the remains of a family home of the first century, possibly that of Flavius Clemens. Christians of the fourth century, wishing to honour Clement who, according to tradition, had been deported to Crimea and martyred, built a church in his honour over the Roman house-church. Little remains of this church, which was destroyed in the sack of Rome in 1084 by the Normans, apart from a number of frescoes depicting the life of Clement and a shrine in honour of Saints Cyril and Methodius, the apostles of the Slavs who are believed to have brought relics of Clement to Rome. Saints Cyril and Methodius, with St Benedict, are the Patrons of Europe. This building was rediscovered in 1857 by the Irish Dominican, Father Mullooly.

The upper church, built in 1108 in the same style as the previous church, is a model of the basilica style with aisles which are separated by two rows of columns and a great apse and triumphal arch covered in wonderful mosaics of the Vine and the Cross. There is also a remarkable marble floor.

S. STEFANO ROTONDO – ST STEPHEN IN THE ROUND
Via S. Stefano Rotondo, 7 (near Irish College).
08.30-13.00; 14.00-16.00; Summer: 08.30-13.00; 16.00-18.30; Saturday 08.30-12.30.
The original church, built in the fifth century, had three concentric walls with transepts on a Greek cross plan. The church was restored and very much changed in the middle of the fifteenth century.

Tomb of Donnchadh, son of Brian Boru
On the left side is a tablet indicating the burial site of Brian Boru's son, Donnchadh. King Brian and his son, Murchad, were killed at the Battle of Clontarf in 1014 – the decisive battle that brought Viking power to an end in Ireland. Another son, Donnchadh, led Brian's victorious army

back to Munster. The following decades saw the decline of the Dal gCais dynasty and after his defeat in 1058 at the Battle of Sliab gCrot in Tipperary by the King of Leinster, Donnchadh went on pilgrimage to Rome were he died in 1064.

PONTIFICAL IRISH COLLEGE, Colaiste na nGaedheal,
Via dei SS. Quattro, 1.
(See p. 129).

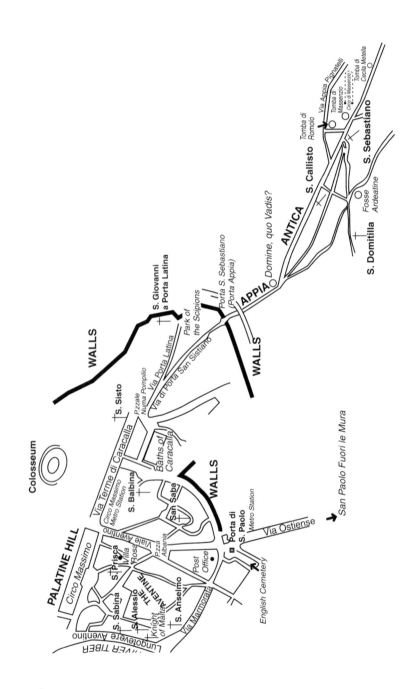

ITINERARY D

CIRCUS MAXIMUS – CATACOMBS – BASILICA OF ST PAUL OUTSIDE THE WALLS

Circus Maximus (Circo Massimo) – Baths of Caracalla –
Church of St Sabina Monastery of St Anselmo –
Basilica of St John at the Latin Gate – Basilica of St Sebastian –
Catacombs of St Sebastian – Church of St Domitilla –
Church of St Calixtus Basilica of St Paul Outside the Walls

CIRCUS MAXIMUS
Metro B, Station Circo Massimo.
Rome's ancient race course, the first and largest circus, or stadium, where horse races and chariot races took place, was begun about 326 BC. It could accommodate over 15,000 spectators. The stadium was in use as a race course and as an arena for extravagant and bloody games with wild animals until 549 AD. The area is now a public park.

TERME DI CARACALLA – BATHS OF CARACALLA
Via delle Terme di Caracalla.
Sunday and Monday 09.00-14.00;
Tuesday-Saturday 09.00-19.00; Winter: 09.00-15.00.
Second only in size to the Baths of Diocletian and named after the emperor who began their construction in 212 AD, the Caracalla Baths were ornate complexes adorned with mosaics and art and were important in the life of the Romans. After exercises the bather first entered the sauna-like *caldarium,* in reality a vapour bath, which was followed by a visit to the cooler *tepidarium,* and finally the swimming pool of the *frigidarium.* There were many facilities for games and various exercises. Until recently, open-air operas were performed among the ruins of the caldarium.

S. SABINA, PIAZZA DI S. PIETRO D'ILLIRIA
06.30-12.45; 15.30-19.00.

Opposite the Circo Massimo is the Aventine Hill. Passing a rose garden, which is beautiful when in bloom, you come to Via di S. Sabine with its famous orange orchard and further on is the site of an early Christian church of the fifth century. Pope Honorius III gave the site to St Dominic in 1219. In the portico of the present building, the door on the left has carved panels in cypress which date from the fifth century. One scene is believed to be the oldest image of the crucifixion. The interior of the church is a superb example of a fifth-century basilica and is based on that of Ravenna. There are many ancient fragments from previous buildings and there are frescoes and paintings which represent scenes from the history of the Dominicans. There is a beautiful thirteenth-century cloister and in the convent is the room where St Dominic died. It is now a chapel. Two Irish Dominicans, Michael Cardinal Brown and Damian Byrne, have served as Masters General of the Order.

S. ANSELMO – MONASTERY OF ST ANSELM
Piazza dei Cavalieri di Malta, 5.

Leaving S. Sabina, on the right is the approach to the Piazza and S. Anselmo, an international house of the Benedictine Order and the residence of the Abbot Primate of the Confederation of Benedictine Monasteries. It is also the home of the Pontifical Athenaeum with its specialist Liturgical Institute. Mass with Gregorian chant is celebrated each Sunday during the academic year at 08.30. On the right of the piazza is the residence of the Grand Master of the Knights of Malta. Through the keyhole of the main door there is an interesting view of the Dome of the Basilica of St Peter.

S. GIOVANNI A PORTA LATINA – BASILICA OF ST JOHN OF THE LATIN GATE
Via di Porta Latina.

This fifth-century basilica was restored to its original appearance in the late 1930s. The Cycle of frescoes, though damaged in part, are of exceptional importance in the history of Christian art. The basilica has been a Titular Church since 1517 and one of its Cardinal Titulars was Cardinal Mc Rory of Armagh.

The lectern, which was restored after the Second Vatican Council, shows one of the roof tiles of the original church carrying a stamp of the Emperor Theodoric (495-526).

Close by, immediately inside the Latin Gate is the Tempietto of S. Giovanni in Oleo, a small octagonal church that traditionally marks the spot where the Evangelist St John is said to have stepped out unharmed from a cauldron of boiling oil.

S. SEBASTIANO – BASILICA OF ST SEBASTIAN
Via Appia Antica.
Bus 218 from St Piazza S. Giovanni in Laterano.
One of the seven pilgrim churches, it was originally dedicated to Saints Peter and Paul whose bodies had been interred for a while in underground tombs during the persecution of the Christians under the Emperor Valerian. The church was later named after the martyr Sebastian who was killed by arrows during the persecution by Diocletian in 288.

CATACOMBS OF ST SEBASTIAN
Via Appia Antica.
Bus 218 from Piazza S. Giovanni in Laterano.
This catacomb was never forgotten and was a temporary resting place for the bodies of St Peter and St Paul during the Valerian persecution in the middle of the third century. This burial area was the first to be called a catacomb (ad catacumbas, down by the dip, cave, hollow). Closed on Thursdays.

CHURCH OF ST DOMITILLA
Via delle Sette Chiese.
Bus 218 from Piazza S. Giovanni in Laterano.
The most ancient Christian burial place in Rome and among the most extensive catacombs. The catacombs contain over 900 inscriptions and many paintings, including what is believed to be the first representation of the Good Shepherd. Closed on Tuesdays.

CHURCH OF ST CALIXTUS
Via Appia Antica.
Bus 218 from Piazza S. Giovanni in Laterano.
These catacombs were the first rediscovered in 1849. They date from the end of the second century and are the largest in Rome. They were the official burial places of the Bishops of Rome and they contain the tombs of some of the early Popes and of many martyrs. The faith of the early Christians is depicted in the numerous paintings of bread, fish, Jonah, Christ and other biblical scenes. Closed on Wednesdays.

S. PAOLO FUORI DALLE MURA, BASILICA OF ST PAUL OUTSIDE THE WALLS,
Via Ostiense. 07.00-18.30. Metro B, Station S. Paolo.
St Paul was martyred ca. 67 and it is believed that he was buried on the site of the present basilica. A small church already existed when, towards the end of the fourth century, Pope Damasus began the construction of a large basilica in honour of the martyred Apostle. This building underwent many changes and additions and was destroyed in a great fire on 15 July 1823. At the time of the reconstruction of the building by Leo XIII, excavations uncovered a first-century tomb and an inscription dating from the time of Constantine which is dedicated to 'Paul, Apostle and Martyr'. The completed basilica was consecrated by Pope Pius IX in 1854. The new building is an exact copy of the original plan and contains the surviving triumphal arch of the fifth-century building. Its pattern is based on the old Roman basilica style. The Holy Door, opened each Jubilee Year, is the restored bronze door of the previous basilica and the mosaic of Christ and the portraits of the Popes are also reconstructions of the originals. Underneath the portraits of the Popes are medallions in honour of great founders of churches, among whom is St Patrick.

On the right, untouched by the fire, are the original early thirteenth century cloisters of the adjoining Benedictine monastery. They are, in part, the work of the Vassalletti family, the famous mosaic artists. (Daily 09.00-13.00 and 15.00-18.00).

Scriptural reflections during visit to the Basilica of St Paul:

... Saul approved of their killing him (Stephen). That day a severe persecution began against the church in Jerusalem, and all except the apostles were scattered throughout the countryside of Judea and Samaria. Devout men buried Stephen and made loud lamentation over him. But Saul was ravaging the church by entering house after house; dragging off both men and women, he committed them to prison. (Acts 8:1-3)

Meanwhile, Saul, still breathing threats and murder against the disciples of the Lord, went to the high priest and asked him for letters to the synagogues at Damascus, so that if he found any who belonged to the Way, men or women, he might bring them bound to Jerusalem. Now as he was going along and approaching Damascus, suddenly a light from heaven flashed around him. He fell to the ground and heard a voice saying to him, 'Saul, Saul, why do you persecute me?' He asked, 'Who are you, Lord?' The reply came, 'I am Jesus, whom you are persecuting. But get up and enter the city, and you will be told what you are to do.' ... But the Lord said to Ananias, 'Go, for he (Paul) is an instrument whom I have chosen to bring my name before Gentiles and kings and before the people of Israel. I myself will show him how much he must suffer for the sake of my name.' (Acts 9:1-16)

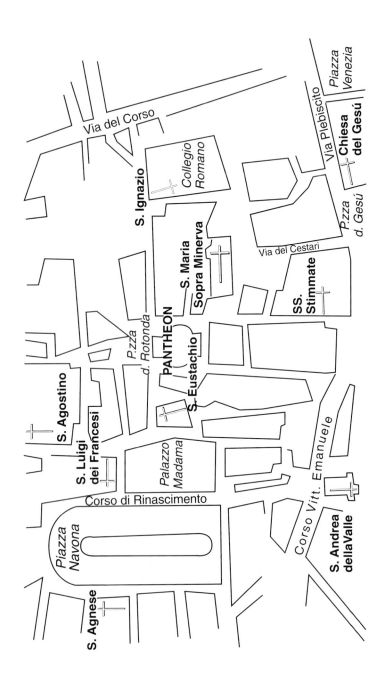

ITINERARY E

PIAZZA VENEZIA – GESÚ – PANTHEON – PIAZZA NAVONA
Church of St Marco – Church of the Gesú – Church of St Ignatius –
Church of St Mary Sopra Minerva – The Pantheon – Church of St Louis –
Church of St Augustine – Piazza Navona – Church of St Andrew

S. MARCO – CHURCH OF ST MARK
Piazza S. Marco.
(off Piazza Venezia, on the right).
This church, for Venetians living in Rome, is dedicated to the Evangelist St Mark. It is said that he wrote his Gospel while living in a house on the Capitoline Hill. The basilica is also dedicated to Pope St Mark who lived here. The present building, which has been rebuilt and changed many times, contains foundations from this period. The interior of the building, approached by steps, retains the form of the classical basilica. The original church was the first parish church in Rome to be built in this form.

GESÚ – CHURCH OF THE GESÚ
Piazza del Gesú. Near Piazza Venezia.
08.00-12.30; 16-30-19.00.
Leaving Piazza Venezia by the Via del Plebiscito, you arrive at the Gesú Church, the church of the Society of Jesus, founded by St Ignatius of Loyola at the time of the Counter Reformation. This Baroque Jesuit church was completed in 1584. In the vault of the nave is the famous fresco by Baciccia, *Triumph of the name of Jesus.* In the transept on the left is the ornate tomb of Ignatius of Loyola. The altar over the tomb is adorned with silver, gilt marble columns and above the altar is the Trinity group with a globe, the largest known piece of lapis lazuli. The church also has the Shrine of St Francis Xavier, with a reliquary containing a relic

of his arm. The rooms where St Ignatius lived from 1544 until he died in 1556 are to the right side of the façade of the church.

S. IGNAZIO – CHURCH OF ST IGNATIUS

Piazza di S. Ignazio. 07.30-12.30; 16.00-19.15.
Crossing the Corso Vittorio Emanuele and following the signs you reach the spacious and highly adorned church with Pozzo's famous vault in the nave and the painted 'dome', which is actually an optical illusion. The building was begun in 1626 to commemorate the canonisation of St Ignatius of Loyola. Various works of art celebrate the triumph of the Saint and the missionary activity of the Jesuits. In the right transept is the chapel of the tomb of St Aloysius Gonzaga. St Robert Bellarmine is buried in the third chapel on the right.

S. MARIA SOPRA MINERVA – CHURCH OF ST MARY ABOVE MINERVA

Piazza della Minerva.
07.30-12.00; 16.00-19.00.
A small church stood on the site of a temple to Minerva before the present Gothic church was begun in 1280 by the brothers Ristoro and Sisto, members of the Dominican Order of Preachers. Though much changed since then, the building remains the only Gothic church in Rome and contains the tombs of many famous people. Under the high altar is the tomb of St Catherine of Siena, Doctor of the Church and Patroness of Italy, who interceded with the Popes during the exile in Avignon and who died in 1380. The monument on the left of the high altar is the tomb of the immortal Fra Angelico. In between these is the figure of *The Risen Christ* with cross, partly attributed to Michelangelo.

In front of the Church is a marble elephant by Bernini, supporting one of the smallest extant Egyptian obelisks. The obelisk dates from the sixth century BC.

THE PANTHEON

Piazza della Rotonda.
09.00-16.30; Sun. 09.00-13.00.
The Pantheon, a pagan temple to 'all the gods', is probably the most famous and best preserved of all the monuments of the Empire. The original temple was built by Agrippa in 27 BC to commemorate Octavian's victory over Anthony and Cleopatra. It was restored after the fire of 80 AD by Domitian and the stamped bricks indicate that the present building is that restored by Hadrian in the early second century. After years of having been abandoned and plundered by the barbarians it became the Church of Mary of the Martyrs.

The temple is a perfect circle. The height and diameter of the interior are identical, that is, 43.3 metres. If the circumference of the dome were continued downward, it would form a sphere touching the ground. The dome is windowless and is a single concrete cast, open to the sky. It was once plated in gold and is more than one metre larger than the dome of St Peter's. On the left, beyond the nineteenth-century tombs of King Umberto I and Queen Margherita, is the tomb of the great artist Raphael, with the well-known tribute by Alexander Pope: 'Living, great Nature feared he might outvie her works, and dying, fears herself may die.'

Tradition has it that Pope Urban VIII melted the bronze ceiling of the portico to cast the bronze 'baldacchino', or canopy, of the papal altar in St Peter's, a tradition now immortalised by the saying: *Quod non fecerunt barbari fecerunt Barberini!* (What the barbarians did not do, the Barberini did!)

S. LUIGI DEI FRANCESI – CHURCH OF ST LOUIS
Piazza di S. Luigi dei Francesi.
09.00-12.30; 16.00-18.00.
Built in the sixteenth century, the Church of St Louis is the French national church in Rome and is famous for the three great Caravaggio paintings in the first chapel at the top of the left aisle. The paintings depict the call of Matthew the tax-collector (left), St Matthew and the Angel (centre), and the Martyrdom of St Matthew.

S. AGOSTINO, CHURCH OF ST AUGUSTINE
Piazza S. Agostino. 07.30-12.00; 16.30-19.30.
Built towards the end of the fifteenth century with stone taken from the Colosseum, this early Renaissance church is dedicated to St Augustine, who wrote the *Confessions*. The tomb of St Monica, Augustine's mother, is in the chapel to the left of the sanctuary. On the third pillar on the north side is a fresco of Isaiah by Raphael. Two angels on the High Altar are by Bernini, as is the second chapel in the north aisle. In the last chapel in this aisle is Caravaggio's famous and beautiful *Madonna of Loreto*, depicting the Madonna with Child receiving pilgrims.

PIAZZA NAVONA
Originally a stadium built by Domitian, it was inaugurated in 86 AD and could hold 30,000 spectators. It has in turn been used for games, as a market place and during the seventeenth to nineteenth centuries it was flooded for aquatic games. It has a popular Christmas market.

The central fountain is of sculpted rocks and vegetation by Bernini, supporting an obelisk brought from Egypt by Domitian. The four great figures represent the rivers Danube, Ganges, Nile and River Plate, and they stand for the four continents, Europe, Asia, Africa and America.

The church of St Agnes – with the large dome on the side of the Piazza near the fountain – occupies the site which tradition marks as the place where St Agnes, the young Virgin, was martyred. Weekdays 17.00-19.00. Sunday 10.00-13.00.

S. ANDREA DELLA VALLE – CHURCH OF ST ANDREW
Corso Vittorio Emanuele.
07.30-12.00; 16.30-19.30.
The dome of St Andrew's is just a little smaller than that of St Peter's. The seventeenth-century Baroque church contains papal tombs of the Piccolomini Popes which were transferred from St Peter's in 1614. It was in this church in 1847 that Fr Ventura gave his two-day long eulogy on the death of Daniel O'Connell. The Church is also the setting for Act I of Puccini's opera *Tosca*.

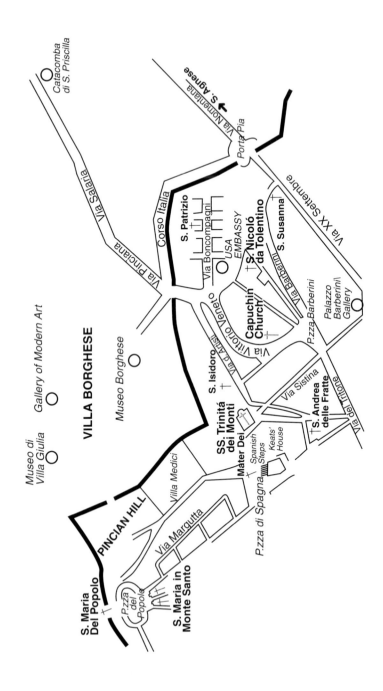

ITINERARY F

PIAZZA DI SPAGNA – NATIONAL GALLERY (PALAZZO BARBERINI) – ST ISIDORE'S – ST PATRICK'S – VILLA BORGHESE MUSEUM – CATACOMBS OF ST PRISCILLA

Piazza del Popolo – Piazza di Spagna – Piazza and Palazzo Barberini – Church of St Isidore's – Church of St Patrick – Villa Borghese Museum – Villa Giulia – Porta Pia – Catacombs of St Agnes – Catacombs of St Priscilla – Villa Ada

PIAZZA DEL POPOLO
Metro Line A, Station Flaminio.
Situated near the Pincian Hill, the piazza has recently been cleaned and is now a pedestrian area. The piazza has four churches and a striking fountain and obelisk dating from the thirteenth century BC, which Caesar Augustus brought to Rome just before the birth of Christ. The gate is the entry from the Via Flaminia which was one of the ancient Roman roads to the north.

To the right of the gate is the famous church, S. Maria del Popolo, said to be the site of Nero's tomb, which was built towards the end of the fifteenth-century. In the church to the left of the choir are two famous paintings by Caravaggio: the *Execution of St Peter* and the *Conversion of St Paul.* In the first and third chapels on the right aisle are Pinturicchio's *Nativity* and a *Madonna,* respectively.

PIAZZA DI SPAGNA – SPANISH STEPS
Metro Line A, Station Piazza di Spagna.
Leaving Piazza del Popolo by Via del Babuino, you arrive at the Piazza di Spagna, so named because of the location nearby of the Spanish Embassy

to the Holy See. The Piazza is famous for the Spanish Steps, a sweeping flight of 137 steps built at the beginning of the eighteenth century. It is a mecca for tourists. At the top of the steps is the church of the Holy Trinity (Trinitá dei Monti) from which there is a marvellous view of the city. In the centre of the Piazza is the attractive boat-like fountain. To the right of the steps is the house where the poet Keats lived and died. It is now the Keats-Shelley Memorial House and has a library and museum, with some autographed letters and books. It is dedicated to the Romantics who spent time in Italy.

At the southern end of the Piazza stands a column which is now crowned with a statue of Our Lady, commemorating the definition of the doctrine of the Immaculate Conception of Mary. The Pope comes to the area every year on 8 December and lays a garland on the column.

Nearby is the large building by Borromini (1622) that houses the Congregation for the Evangelization of Peoples, which supervises the missionary activity of the Catholic Church. The building once housed the College for the Propagation of the Faith. St Oliver Plunkett (1629-1681), on the completion of his post-graduate studies, was Professor of Theology there until his appointment as Archbishop of Armagh in 1669. Paul Cullen (1803-1878), later Archbishop of Dublin and Ireland's first Cardinal, became Rector of the College in 1849.

PIAZZA BARBERINI
Walking along Via Sistina at the top of the Spanish Steps you arrive at Piazza Barberini. In the centre of the Piazza is Triton's Fountain by Bernini, finished in 1640. Four frolicking dolphins support a triton who is seated on a shell. As you face the fountain, on the street to the right, Via Barberini 18, is the Palazzo Barberini, the work of Maderna, Borromini and finished by Bernini in 1633. It now houses the National Gallery of Ancient Art, a collection of paintings of the thirteenth to sixteenth centuries, by many of the great masters such as Titian, 'El Greco', Holbein, Fra Angelico, and Caravaggio. 09.00-21.00; Saturday 09.00-24.00; Sunday and holidays 09.00-20.00. Closed Monday. Entrance ITL 8.000.

S. ISIDORO – CHURCH OF ST ISIDORE OFM (Irish Franciscans)
Via degli Artisti, 41. Tel. 06-488-5359
Reached by steps from the Via Veneto, the College of St Isidore was founded in 1625 by the famous scholar, theologian and Irishman, Luke Wadding OFM (1588-1657). (See p.128)

S. PATRIZIO – CHURCH OF ST PATRICK OSA (Irish Augustinians)

Via Boncompagni, 31. Tel. 06-488-5716.
The Irish Augustinians established their first College in Rome in 1656.
(See p. 134)

VILLA BORGHESE MUSEUM

Piazzale Scipione Borghese, 5 (near Porta del Popolo, behind the Pincio).
Tuesday-Saturday: Entry at 09.00, 11.00, 13.00,15.00, 17.00 and 19.00;
Sunday and holidays: Entry at 09.00, 11.00, 13.00, 15.00, and 17.00.
Closed Mondays.
Booking is compulsory: Tel. 06-32810.
Once the villa of Cardinal Scipione Borghese, this seventeenth-century
museum reopened in 1997 after fourteen years of restoration work. The
museum is second only to the Vatican Museum in the number of
priceless works on display, despite the fact that Napoleon removed so
many masterpieces to the Louvre. On the ground floor is the unrivalled
collection of sculpture by Bernini and Canova. In the upstairs galleries
are works by Rubens, Caravaggio, Raphael and Titian. The villa is set in
the famous Borghese Gardens. The gardens were bought by the State in
1902 and are much used by the public who enjoy the many fountains,
statues and fine trees.

VILLA GIULIA

Viale delle Belle Arti, Piazza Villa Giulia, 9.
09.00-19.00; Sunday and holidays 09.00-14.00.
Closed Monday. Entrance ITL 8.000.
Villa Giulia was built by the last of the Renaissance Pope Julius III. Since
the last century it has been a museum of Etruscan art, ceramics and
culture.

PORTA PIA

Piazzale di Porta Pia.
One of Michelangelo's last designs, the gate was built by Pius IV in 1561
and reconstructed in the middle of the last century. Outside the gate, to
the right, now marked by a monument, is the place where the Italian
troops breached the Wall and entered Rome on September 1870, thus
ending the temporal power of the Popes. The taking of Rome also
brought the deliberations of the Vatican I Council to an end.

CATACOMBS OF ST AGNES

Via Nomentana, 349 (beyond Porta Pia).

Bus 60, 62 from Piazza Venezia; Bus 36 from Termini.

The church, dating from the fourth century, contains the tomb of the young virgin martyr, St Agnes, commissioned by the Emperor Constantine. In the catacombs there are many inscriptions and some of the loculi are intact.

Daily 09.00-12.00; 16.00-18.00.

CATACOMBS OF ST PRISCILLA

Via Salaria, 430.

Bus 319 from Termini.

Interesting for its third-century Greek Funerary Chapel and biblical frescoes. Closed Monday.

VILLA ADA

Villa Ada, opposite the Catacombs of St Priscilla, is one of the largest parks in Rome. It was once the private residence of Victor Emmanuel III, King of Italy from 1900 to 1946.

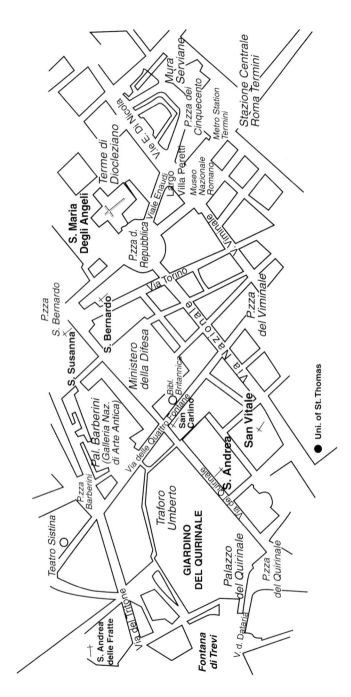

ITINERARY G

TERMINI STATION – VIA NAZIONALE – QUIRINAL PALACE – CHURCH OF ST MARY OF VICTORY

Piazza dei Cinquecento (Termini Station) – Baths of Diocletian –
Via Nazionale – University of St Thomas (Angelicum) –
Piazza of the Quirinal Palace – Church of St Andrew near the Quirinale –
Church of St Mary of Victory

PIAZZA DE CINQUECENTO, TERMINI STATION

The large square in front of the main Railway Station Termini is named after 500 Italian soldiers who died in Africa in 1887. To the left are walls built in the fourth century BC to defend the city against the invading Gauls.

BATHS OF DIOCLETIAN

Near the Piazza della Repubblica are the largest of the Roman baths, which were completed in 306 AD and could accommodate over 3000 people at one time. In 1561 Michelangelo built the Church of S. Maria degli Angeli (St Mary of the Angels) where the tepidarium stood. The church is used for official occasions and contains the tombs of many famous Italians – Carlo Moratta (d. 1713), Salvator Rosa (d. 1673), Marshal Armando Diaz (d. 1928). There is a remarkable meridian in the floor (1703), used for many years to calculate the time in Rome. To the right of the church is the National Museum which contains a large and important collection of classical sculptures and statuary.

VIA NAZIONALE

Via Nazionale is a busy main street with a variety of fashion boutiques.

UNIVERSITY OF ST THOMAS – ANGELICUM

At the end of Via Nazionale, on the left, is the Dominican 'Angelicum' University which is named after St Thomas Aquinas, the 'Angelic Doctor'. A centre for undergraduate and postgraduate Catholic and Ecumenical studies for lay, religious and clerical students, there have been, and are, many Irish professors on the staff. Michael Browne OP and Conleth Kerins OP were Rectors of the University. Michael Browne later became a member of the College of Cardinals and was appointed Theologian to the Pope Pius XII. Many Irish students attend the University.

PIAZZA OF THE QUIRINAL PALACE

At the end of the Via Nazionale, on the right, built on the highest of the hills of ancient Rome, is the Palace begun by Gregory XIII in 1574 as a papal summer residence. It was a royal residence for the Kings of Italy between 1870 and 1946, and is now the official home of the President of the Republic. The Quirinal Pauline Chapel is a reproduction of the Sistine Chapel.

S. ANDREA AL QUIRINALE – CHURCH OF ST ANDREW NEAR THE QUIRINALE
Via del Quirinale
This marble and gilded church with its oval interior was built by Bernini in 1678.

S. MARIA DELLA VITTORIA – CHURCH OF ST MARY OF VICTORY
Via XX Settembre
Built in honour of Our Lady, the church is now famous for Bernini's remarkable statue of St Teresa of Avila in ecstasy.

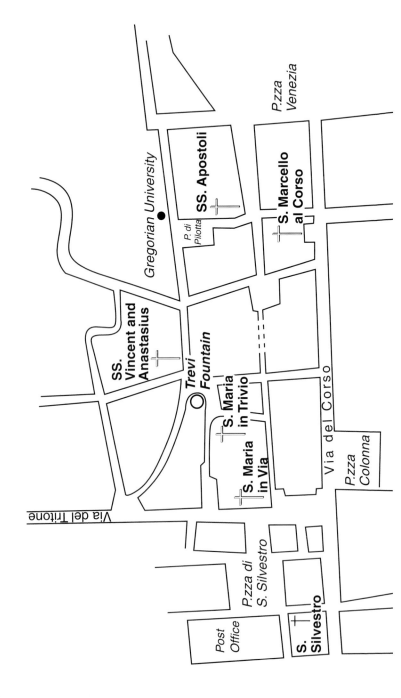

ITINERARY H

S. SILVESTRO – TREVI FOUNTAIN –
CHURCH OF THE APOSTOLES – CHURCH OF ST MARCELLUS
Church of St Silvestro – The Trevi Fountain –
Church of Saints Vincent and Anastasius – Church of St Mary in Trivio –
Gregorian University and Biblical Institute –
Church of the Apostles – Church of St Marcellus

S. SILVESTRO IN CAPITE - CHURCH OF ST SYLVESTER
Piazza San Silvestro.
The original church on the site was built in the eighth century by the brothers Pope Stephen II and Pope Paul I on the site of their father's home as a sanctuary for the relics of the saints and martyrs who had been buried in the catacombs. The Longobards had laid siege to Rome and its environs at the time, and it became necessary to transfer many of these revered remains to safety within the walls of the city.

The present basilica was built at the end of the sixteenth century by the Poor Clare Sisters. The decoration of the basilica was carried out at intervals throughout the seventeenth century. This sacred place has a rich artistic and archaeological heritage. The entire property was confiscated by the state at the time of the Unification of Italy in 1870. The greater part of the monastery became the Central Post Office. The basilica was reopened for public worship in 1885 and entrusted to the pastoral care of the Pallottines by Pope Leo XIII, 'to be used in particular for providing facilities for people using the English language.' There are many services available for English-speaking residents and visitors. There is an information office in the basilica (on the right as you enter), and guided tours are available on request.

THE TREVI FOUNTAIN
Piazza di Trevi.
Fed by water from the aqueduct called the Acqua Vergine, which was built by the Emperor Augustus in the year 19 BC, the Trevi is a large and impressive fountain. Originally planned by Bernini, the present fountain was completed in 1762. In the midst of cascading waters, the centrepiece consists of Neptune on his chariot drawn by marine horses who follow the Tritons. An old custom urges the visitor to toss a coin into the fountain whilst making a wish to return to Rome. The fountain is cleaned each Monday morning and the coins are collected for charity.

SS. VINCENZO E ANASTASIO – CHURCH OF SAINTS VINCENT AND ANASTASIUS
Near Trevi Fountain
This Baroque church, rebuilt in 1630, contains the remains of some of the Popes who died in the nearby Quirinal Palace.

S. MARIA IN TRIVIO – CHURCH OF ST MARY IN TRIVIO
To the left of the Trevi Fountain, this small baroque church features a well known fifteenth-century painting of Our Lady over the high altar. On the left is the tomb of the founder of the Priests of the Precious Blood, St Gaspar del Bufalo, who died in 1837.

GREGORIAN UNIVERSITY AND BIBLICAL INSTITUTE
Piazza della Pilota.
When you leave the Trevi Fountain behind, you soon come to Piazza della Pilota with the Jesuit directed Gregorian University and Biblical Institute, centres of theological and biblical studies for members of the clergy, religious and laity. There have been Irish priests and sisters on the staff of the University over the years and many Irish priests and religious have studied there.

SS. APOSTOLI – CHURCH OF THE APOSTLES
Piazza dei Santi Apostoli.
Built in 560 to celebrate the defeat of the Goths, the church was almost completely rebuilt in the early eighteenth century. It is dedicated to the Apostles Philip and James, whose relics are preserved in the confessio, approached by the steps in front of the sanctuary. In the second cloister on the left of the façade is a memorial to Michelangelo whose body rested here before being brought to Florence.

S. Marcello al Corso – Church of St Marcellus

Via del Corso.

Built on the site of a Christian home, the present Baroque church replaced the one destroyed by fire in 1519 and is dedicated to Pope St Marcellus who was martyred by the Emperor Maxentius at the end of the third century. The famous crucifix, recovered from the old church, is an object of special veneration and was carried in procession at the opening of the Second Vatican Council and is usually kept in the second chapel on the right. The church has been in the care of the Servites since 1369.

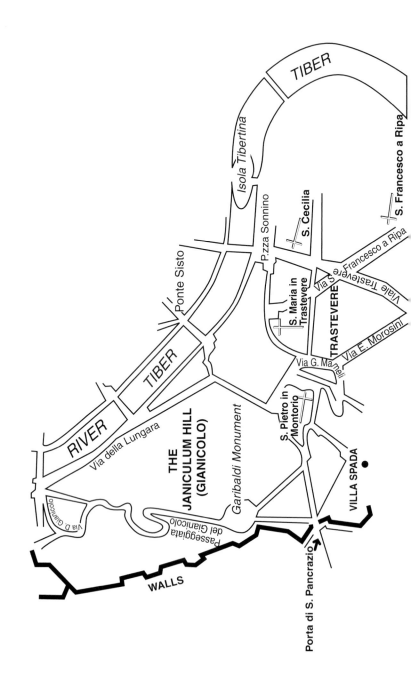

ITINERARY I

TRASTEVERE – JANICULUM HILL
Church of St Cecily – Church of St Mary in Trastevere –
Church of St Francis – Church of St Peter in Montorio –
Villa Spada – The Janiculum

S. CECILIA – CHURCH OF ST CECILY
Piazza di S. Cecilia.
Tram No. 8 from Largo Argentino to Piazza Sonnino.
According to tradition, Cecily was martyred on this site, which was her home, ca. 300. Her body was removed to the Catacombs of St Callistus. Following a dream, Pope Paschal discovered her body intact and incorrupt 500 years later and re-buried it in the new church he had built. The tomb was re-opened in 1599 and the body was still intact. The sculpture by Stefano Maderno, which now lies beneath the altar, is based on the exact form and position of the body when the tomb was re-opened in 1599. The body of her husband, Valerian, lies near her. The church has notable mosaics and floors, and the apse is from the original church.

S. MARIA IN TRASTEVERE – CHURCH OF ST MARY IN TRASTEVERE
Piazza di S. Maria in Trastevere. Near Piazza Sonnino.
It is believed that this church was the first in Rome to be dedicated to Our Lady. The structure of the present building dates from the twelfth century – it has been renovated a number of times – and the façade has mosaics from the twelfth and thirteenth centuries. The building has naves separated by ancient columns. There are some famous mosaics on the vault, depicting the life of Christ and the Apostles. The lower mosaics are the Cavallini mosaics, done in 1291, which depict events in the life of Our Lady.

S. FRANCESCO A RIPA – CHURCH OF ST FRANCIS
Via di S. Francesco a Ripa.
There was a hospice attached to a Benedictine church here in the thirteenth century. When St Francis came to Rome this is where he stayed; you can request to see the well-preserved cell. In the chapel near the sacristy is Bernini's renowned sculpture of the widow Blessed Ludovica Albertone who died in 1533.

S. PIETRO IN MONTORIO – CHURCH OF ST PETER IN MONTORIO
Via Garibaldi, Janiculum.
The present church was built by Sixtus IV with financial contributions from the Kings of Portugal, France and Spain for a community of Franciscans led by the Pope's confessor, Blessed Amedeo da Silva. In the courtyard to the right of the church is the temple of Bramante, built in 1500 by Ferdinand and Isabella of Spain, in thanksgiving for the birth of their son through the intercession of Blessed Amedeo. The temple is the first Renaissance building in Rome and marks the site which was long believed to be that of the martyrdom of St Peter.

Raphael's masterpiece, *The Transfiguration*, adorned the apse of the church for almost three centuries before being removed to Paris by Napoleon. On its return, it was housed in the Vatican Museum and a copy of Guido Reni's *Martyrdom of St Peter* was put in its place. The first chapel to the right contains Sebastiano del Piombo's fresco, the *Scourging of Christ*, for which Michelangelo is said to have modelled the figure of Christ. The third chapel on the right was built by Pope Julius III and contains *The Conversion of St Paul* by Giorgio Vasari. The second chapel on the left is by Bernini.

The Great Hugh O'Neill left Ireland in 1607 with the intention of travelling to Spain to seek help from the King for a renewed war against England. Since Spain had made peace with England, O'Neill was sent to Rome instead and spent the last eight years of his life there before he died in 1616. The site of his burial is beside the last chapel on the left and is marked by a simple slab. To the right two more elaborate gravestones with Latin inscriptions mark the burial site of one of O'Neill's sons and one of Red Hugh O'Donnell's sons.

VILLA SPADA, EMBASSY OF IRELAND TO THE HOLY SEE
Via Giacomo Medici, I.
Close to the Church of S. Pietro in Montorio is the Villa Spada, the Embassy of Ireland to the Holy See. It was built in 1635-41 by Vincenzo Nobili, a grand-nephew of Pope Julius III. In 1849, the Villa Spada was the last headquarters of Garibaldi, then defending the Roman Republic

against the French. It suffered some damage in the fighting as did the Church of S. Pietro in Montorio. It was acquired by the Government of Ireland in 1946.

THE JANICULUM
From the Garibaldi monument on the Janiculum hill there is a splendid panoramic view of Rome and the hills to the south of Rome.

EXCURSIONS OUTSIDE ROME

The Alban Hills

A series of volcanic hills to the south of Rome, the Alban Hills (*Colli Albani*), encircle the Castelli Romani, a number of typical small Italian towns with famous names such as Castel Gandolfo (the summer residence of the Pope), Frascati, Rocca di Papa, Grottaferrata, Marino, Genzano and Nemi. Many of these towns were damaged during the Second World War. There are also two lovely lakes, Lake Nemi, where the worship of the Goddess Diana flourished, and Lake Albano near Castel Gandolfo.

By Train: Trains from Rome Termini diverge at Ciampino Station for Velletri, Frascati, and Albano Laziale (passing through Marino and Castel Gandolfo).

By Bus: Take Metro Line A from Termini to Station Anagnina and then a blue bus to desired destination.

Assisi

A two-hour train-trip from Rome, this unique medieval Italian hilltop town, though ravaged by the earthquakes of 1997, is worth a visit. The prayerful spirit and charism of St Francis (1182-1226) touches the pilgrim of today.

A suggested timetable for a one day visit to Assisi: **By Train:** Leave from Termini on the 07.10 train destined for Ancona. The ticket will indicate the number of the train and the large yellow schedule screens and the display screen at the beginning of each platform will indicate the destination. Validate the ticket in the orange stamping machine at the entrance to the platform. Leave the train at Foligno and take the local train to Assisi, a 15-minute trip. At Assisi Station buy two bus tickets and walk to the Portiuncola Basilica for a visit. When finished, take a bus to Assisi and go to *Parcheggio B* to visit S. Damiano. After the visit return to *Parcheggio B* and climb the steps to the town. Visit S. Chiara Church (St Clare's Church), Chiesa Nuova (St Francis' house) and then continue to the Basilica of S. Francesco. Following this visit go to *Parcheggio A* (below Basilica of St Francis) and take the bus to the station. A train leaves shortly after 17.00 for the two-hour return trip to Rome.

An alternative train trip, which is somewhat faster, but more expensive, is to take the 08.00 **ES** (Eurostar) train from Rome which goes to Assisi (its destination is Perugia): seats must be pre-booked. There is a return **IC** (intercity) train direct to Rome, departing from Assisi at 18.20.

By Bus: There is a daily service to Assisi. Buses leave from the bus park near the metro and railway station Tiburtina at 07.15. Tickets can be purchased on bus. Get off at S. Maria degli Angeli (Portiuncola) and after the visit buy a bus ticket in a tobacconist shop for the trip up the hill to Assisi.

EUR
Penultimate stop on Metro Line B, direction Laurentina.
Mussolini planned to hold a world fair on this site, the Universal Exhibition of Rome (EUR), but because of the Second World War, it did not take place. War-damaged buildings were restored and in 1952 many government offices and museums were transferred from Rome. The Museo della Civilitá Romana (Museum of Roman Civilisation), Piazza G. Agnelli 10, has many interesting plaster casts depicting the history and life of ancient Rome. In Room XXXVI there is a famous model of the city as it was in the fourth century.

Ostia Antica
Ostia Antica, which takes its name from the Latin word *ostium*, meaning mouth, is where the river Tiber used to meet the sea. The present remains of the town date from the fourth century BC. Originally a walled city, its main trade was extracting salt from the nearby marshes. It later became the main port of Rome and a great commercial city, responsible for most of the food provisions of Rome. During the days of the Empire it was also the harbour of the fleet. The decline of Ostia as a commercial centre began when Constantine favoured the newer port at Porto. An epidemic of malaria hastened the decline. In 387 AD St Augustine was ready to sail to Africa with his mother, St Monica, when she became ill and died soon after in Ostia.

The sands that covered the ruins helped to preserve them. Excavations carried out in this century present a clear plan of a great part of the old city and give an idea of what life was like in a busy first and second century commercial centre. In some houses it is possible to see the original marble and mosaic floors. If a trip to Pompeii is not possible, Ostia is well worth a visit.

From Termini take the Metro Line B for Laurentina, get off at Station Piramide or S. Paolo. Take the train for Lido, and get off at Ostia Antica. Cross the bridge – the entrance to the excavations is on the left. Admission is free for those under 18 years of age and over 60 – bring a photocopy of passport. The weekly metrebus ticket is valid for the train journey.

Tivoli
Take Metro Line B to the end at Rebbibia, buy two bus tickets, one for the trip to Tivoli and one for the return.

Villa D'Este is renowned for its garden and 500 remarkable fountains (09.00-dusk. Closed Mondays). It was built in 1550, partly with material taken from the ruins of the nearby extraordinary summer villa of the Emperor Hadrian which was completed in AD 134, who in his later years sought to recapture in stone some of the famous buildings and monuments he had seen on his travels through the Empire.

Section III

Religious Houses and Institutions with Irish Connections

ST ISIDORE'S OFM (IRISH FRANCISCANS)
Via degli Artisti, 41, Rome 00187.
Tel. 06-488-5359; Fax. 06-488-4459.
The College of St Isidore is still used by the Irish Franciscans. Fr Luke
Wadding, from Waterford, arrived in Rome from Spain as an official
Spanish emissary in 1617. He was sent as a theologian to promote the
dogma of the Immaculate Conception of Our Lady. During his time in
Rome he sought to found an Irish Franciscan College. A group of
Spanish Franciscans had begun the establishment of a friary dedicated to
St Isidore of Madrid, Patron of Farmers, who had just been canonised in
1622. Due to financial problems, and difficulty with a reform, the
Spanish friars withdrew and went to live at *Ara Coeli*, the residence of the
Minister General. Fr Wadding was asked by the General to consider
using the building (small church and friary) for the needs of the Irish
Franciscans. It was granted to the Irish Friars by decree of the Minister
General on 13 June 1625. Pope Urban VIII issued the Bull of Foundation
on 20 October. From then on until his death on 18 November 1657,
Wadding laboured to build and extend the College. He also founded,
with Cardinal Ludovisi, the Irish Pastoral College for the Education of
the Irish Diocesan Clergy as well as a Novitiate house for the Irish
Franciscans at Capranica, north of Rome. Wadding's fame as a writer and
critic rests chiefly on his *Annales Ordinis Minorum* and his monumental
edition of Blessed John Dun Scotus on the *Scriptores*. He was also
responsible for having St Patrick placed on the Universal Calendar of the
Church and he represented Ireland on many issues in difficult times.

Major restoration work was done at St Isidore's in 1750. The building
was seized by the invading French forces in 1798-1799 and again in 1810.
On this occasion the College was turned into rented accommodation and
many of the rooms were rented to a group of artists known as the
Nazarenes – hence the name of the street, *Via degli Artisti*. The guardian, Fr
James McCormack, remained in residence and regained control of the
College in October 1814. Following the appointment of Fr Bernard
Doebbing as lecturer and master, the College became a centre of reform of
the Irish friars in the late nineteenth century. Students were normally
trained in theology by lecturers living in the College. Since the Second
World War they began to attend the outside universities in Rome.
Although cut off from Ireland during the Second World War, the College
was able to remain active and is still the main house of formation for the
Irish Franciscans.

The Church of St Isidore has a number of important artistic works and
monuments. Among them are the Chapel of the Immaculate
Conception (painting by Carlo Marrata and sculpture by Bernini), the

tomb slabs of Luke Wadding and Aodh MacAingil, Archbishop of Armagh (d. 1627), a monument to Amelia Curran, artist (sister of Sarah Curran), and the tomb of Octavia Caterina Bryan (who died at nineteen years of age in 1846). For further information on St Isidore's, cf. website: www.geocities.com./Paris/3658.

PONTIFICAL IRISH COLLEGE (COLÁISTE NA NGAEDHEAL)
Via dei SS. Quattro, 1, Rome 00184.
PILGRIMS' OFFICE Tel. 06-772-631
The Irish College, Rome, was founded on 1 January 1628 by the Irish Franciscan, Fr Luke Wadding, and the Roman Cardinal, Ludovico Ludovisi for the education of students for the priesthood in Ireland. Initially, the College was under the care of the Irish Franciscans but when Cardinal Ludovisi died he willed that the College should be placed in the care of the Jesuits. His will was contested by the Franciscans and in February 1635 the Sacred Roman Rota decided that the Cardinal's wishes should be honoured and the College remained under the care of the Jesuits until 1772. When the French entered Rome in 1798 the College was closed and it re-opened after the end of the Napoleonic Wars in 1826. Since that time the Irish College has been cared for by the Irish Bishops and all the Rectors of the College have been Irishmen.

After almost four hundred years, the College continues the work of educating men for the priesthood in Ireland. Nowadays, however, there are fewer seminarians than in the past. Many Irish priests are doing post-graduate studies in the College, together with other priests and Orthodox ministers from around the globe. In all there are over sixty students in the College.

For over a quarter of a century, Irish couples have come to the College to celebrate their marriages and about three hundred couples marry here each year. During the summer, when the seminarians and priests have returned to Ireland, the College is open as a Pilgrim Centre. For about ten weeks each year, from 1 July until 20 September, people from many countries, especially Ireland, stay in the College and benefit from what the College has to offer; a quiet atmosphere in which people can pray, reflect and relax.

The College is always happy to welcome visitors. As you enter the grounds you are asked to follow the signs which lead to the Pilgrims Office. There you will be given some information on the College and made welcome with a cup of tea. You will then be directed to the College Chapel, the Salone and the monument to Daniel O'Connell.

Since the College is home to almost sixty students and priests, you are asked to respect the notices. If you can call the College before you visit (Tel. No. 06-772-631) you will have a better chance of meeting someone who may be able to show you around. Otherwise, you will appreciate that the normal routine of study and work may not allow for individual care for every pilgrim during the Holy Year.

The Monument to Daniel O'Connell

Daniel O'Connell (1775-1847), known in his lifetime as the 'Liberator', was a champion of the cause of Catholic emancipation. He died at Genoa, while on pilgrimage to the Eternal City. On his deathbed he left his body to Ireland, his soul to God and his heart to Rome. His wishes were carried out and his heart placed in a silver container. Within a few years his friend, Charles Bianconi, himself an Italian, commissioned the Italian sculptor Benzoni to carve this monument from Carrara marble. The bas-relief shows O'Connell in the House of Commons refusing to take the Oath of Allegiance.

The Salone

This formal reception room houses a collection of furniture and paintings that have been in the possession of the College for centuries. The collection includes a painting of St Patrick on the Hill of Slane by Sean Keating, an Annunciation from the school of Arezzo and a Crucifixion attributed to Guido Reni.

Other items of interest include a book presented to the College by St Oliver Plunkett and the cross he wore on the day of his execution.

The College Vault

Since 1879 all who died at the College have been buried in the College vault in Campo Verano. Situated almost directly in front of the Chapel in the original part of the cemetery, some twenty six burials have taken place. They include the former Rectors, Kirby, Murphy, O'Riordan, Hagan and McDaid. Seminarians from many dioceses are also buried there, together with a few religious and members of the laity. The list of those interred in the vault is available on request from the Rector for the families of those buried in the vault.

The College Register

The present register began in 1826 and is a record of over 2000 men who have studied in the College since then. Information on particular individuals is available on request from the Rector.

Information
Rector: Monsignor John Fleming
College Office Hours: Monday to Saturday: 08.30-19.30
Tel. 06-772-631; Fax. 06-7726-3323
Sunday Mass: 09.30

LITTLE COMPANY OF MARY LCM
Via S. Stefano Rotondo, 6, Rome 00184. Tel. 06-7047-6780
The specific mission of the Congregation is spiritual assistance to the dying in union with Our Lady at the foot of the Cross. As an apostolic congregation dedicated to the sick and dying, the Sisters exercise their mission primarily through the health-care ministry.

Mary Potter founded the Little Company of Mary in Nottingham, England, in the year 1877. In 1882 she came to Rome to ask the blessing of the Vicar of Christ, Pope Leo XIII, on the Congregation and also to get the Holy See's approval for its constitutions. Mother Potter had intended to return to England but at the Holy Father's invitation she remained and made a foundation in Rome.

On 19 March 1907 the Calvary Hospital at San Stefano Rotondo was opened. Mother Potter soon understood the importance of having the Sisters trained as nurses. The only problem was that training schools did not as yet exist in Italy. To meet the need she opened a nursing training school annexe to the Hospital at San Stefano Rotondo for the training of both Sisters of the Congregation and Italian girls. This was the first nursing training school of its kind in Italy. In 1909 the first group of nurses received their State Diploma. An important aspect of Mother Potter's contribution to the reform was her initiative in heralding a change in the Church's attitude towards maternity nursing by religious sisters. The Sisters were given permission to engage in maternity nursing: this was an exceptional privilege for the Congregation. In 1936 the then Congregation of the Propagation of the Faith, now the Congregation for the Evangelization of Peoples, issued a document stating that the Church was deeply interested in the nursing profession and was most anxious that Religious Sisters take part in maternity nursing.

From its humble beginnings in Nottingham, the Little Company of Mary has now spread to many countries. There are houses in Italy, England, Ireland, Africa, Australia, New Zealand, USA, Korea, The Tonga Islands and Albania.

CONGREGATION OF THE POOR SERVANTS OF THE MOTHER OF GOD
'Mater Dei' Institute, Via San Sebastianello, 16, Roma 00187.
Tel. 06-679-0634

Mater Dei convent, at the foot of the Pincio Hill, was founded in 1886 by Mother Magdalen Taylor, foundress of the Congregation of the Poor Servants of the Mother of God, with the special approbation of His Holiness, Pope Leo XIII. It was the first English convent established in Rome since the Reformation. From the beginning the Church and convent had been, as the Pope wished, a centre of religious activity for English-speaking people in Rome. The guild of Our Lady of Ransom was canonically erected there in 1890 and in January each year the feast of Our Lady Queen of Prophets is celebrated at that shrine.

From 1887 to 1992 the Poor Servants of the Mother of God responded to the needs of those who were spiritually and materially poor through the spiritual and cultural formation of generations of young Italians and English-speaking students. The school, originally founded for English-speaking students, quickly developed into an Italian school for primary and secondary education.

Today part of the building hosts the International Development Law Institute, which trains legal advisors and lawyers for economic development. Participants in the courses come from Third World countries, and financial support is provided by governments and international organizations as well as private sponsors. The Sisters see this work as a continuation of their service to the poor, as Mother Magdalen desired.

As well as teaching English to foreign students, preparing children for the Sacraments and instructing converts, the Sisters are also engaged in the wider church: they work in the Congregation for the Evangelization of Peoples, the Vatican paper *l'Osservatore Romano*, the International Union of Superiors General, and in the European Office of Evangelization 2000.

DOMINICAN SISTERS, VILLA ROSA
Via Terme Deciane, Aventino, Rome 00153. Tel. 06-571-7091

Villa Rosa on the Aventine was purchased by the Dominican Congregation of St Catherine of Siena, of Natal, South Africa, in 1929, while the house was being built as an apartment building. Adjustments were made to the plans to make it suitable as a convent, for example, by the addition of a chapel. It served as a novitiate until 1939; many young Irish women spent their formation years there before going on to mission-work in South Africa.

At the outbreak of World War II, the Roman novitiate moved to

England. A few Irish Sisters remained to look after the house which, during the Nazi occupation of Rome, was declared to be under the protection of the Irish Legation. After the war the future use of the house was in question; the matter was decided by a request from the Vatican that religious houses with rooms to spare should make them available to pilgrims coming to Rome for the Holy Year, 1950.

Thus Villa Rosa became a pensione and for fifty years has provided accommodation for pilgrims and tourists. It has also served as a student house for Dominican Sisters studying in Rome. Since 1998 it has become an international community of English-speaking Dominican Sisters who are teaching, studying or engaged in other apostolates in Rome.

S. CLEMENTE - BASILICA OF ST CLEMENT (IRISH DOMINICANS)

Via S. Giovanni in Laterano 95, Rome 00184. Metro B Station Colosseo
Tel. 06-7045-1018
09.00-12.30; 15.00-18-00

The Basilica, which has been under the care of the Irish Dominicans since 1677, is dedicated to the fourth Pope, St Clement. It has three superimposed buildings. Deep underneath, at first-century street level, there are a number of rooms that are believed to have been part of the Imperial Mint.

Christians of the fourth century, wishing to honour St Clement, who, according to tradition, had been deported to Crimea and martyred, built a Basilica here, on the site of what was possibly an early house-church. This Basilica was abandoned and buried in the twelfth century in order to build a new Basilica at what was by then a much higher street level. Before filling in the old church, the relics of the Saints and the marble fittings were brought up for the new Basilica where they are still housed today. The old fourth-century church was rediscovered during excavations made by Father Joseph Mullooy, of the Irish Dominicans, in 1857.

Father Mulooly's excavations brought to light a wonderful series of mediaeval frescoes dating from the seventh to the eleventh centuries. St Cyril had been buried in this church in the ninth century. There is a shrine to him and to his brother, St Methodius, as well as to the apostles of the Slavs, who are believed to have been responsible for bringing back the relics of St Clement to Rome. Saints Cyril and Methodius, along with St Benedict, St Bridget of Sweden, St Catherine of Siena and St Edith Stein are the co-patrons of Europe.

The upper Basilica was built in the twelfth century in the same style as the fourth-century building. There is a courtyard leading into the Basilica which is divided into two rows of columns with a central nave and two side aisles. The apse, which focuses our attention on the high altar, has wonderful twelfth-century mosaics. The marble cosmatesque floor is contemporary with the Basilica. The frescoes in the chapel of St Catherine of Alexandria were painted in 1425. The rich ceiling and plaster decoration were completed in the eighteenth century. Excavations are still being carried out, and recent discoveries include a baptistery and a fresco of the Madonna, both dating from around the sixth century.

ST PATRICK'S CHURCH OSA (IRISH AUGUSTINIANS)
Via Boncompagni, 31, Rome 00187 Tel. 06-488-5716
One of the seventeen Irish Martyrs beatified in 1992 was the Augustinian, Blessed William Tirry, who was executed in Clonmel on 2 May 1654. A mere two years later the Irish Augustinians were given a College in Rome for the purpose of educating Friars to return to minister in Ireland. This College was called S. Matteo and was on the street that links the two Major Basilicas, St John Lateran and St Mary Major. The Irish Augustinians were there until the French invaded Rome in 1798 and the College and the Church were razed to the ground. On the site of S. Matteo now stands the Redemptorist Church with the world-renowned painting of *Our Mother of Perpetual Help,* by an unknown artist, which was originally in S. Matteo.

After a few years in the wilderness, the Augustinians were given possession of another College and Church called S. Maria in Posterula. This was located on the banks of the River Tiber, not far from St Peter's. The Augustinians were there nearly all the last century. The first Prior was Fr John Rice, brother of Blessed Edmund Rice, founder of the Christian Brothers and the Presentation Brothers. This college and church were requisitioned by the Rome Corporation in 1886 to widen the Tiber and make way for a new bridge, the present Ponte Umberto. In compensation the Augustinians were given a site in Villa Ludovisi and the present St Patrick's College was built in 1892. St Patrick's Church was built some years later in 1910. The architect was Aristide Leonori, a man with a reputation for sanctity, who, besides designing several well-known churches in Rome, was also the architect of Churches in Washington, Chicago, New York and Cairo. The design of St Patrick's is in the fourteenth-century Lombardo-Gothic style. St Patrick's is the Titular Church of the Irish Cardinal.

The church has a thirteenth-century picture of Our Lady of Grace, brought from S. Maria in Posterula. Other items from S. Maria include a marble Holy Communion rail by the Bernini school, now in the Shrine of Our Mother of Good Counsel, Genazzano, and one of the church bells, now in the parish church of Ballyboden, Dublin.

St Patrick's Church also has artistic Stations of the Cross. They are by

Alceo Dossena: each station is carved from a single piece of Carrara marble. They were presented to the church in 1938 by William McAuley, Irish Minister to the Holy See, in memory of his wife, Genevieve.

The apse has a striking mosaic depicting St Patrick on the Hill of Tara, explaining the mystery of the Trinity to King Laoghaire and his court. A mosaic lunette of St Patrick over the main door was inset in March 1937. In 1938 two shrines, one dedicated to St Brigid, the other to St Oliver Plunkett, were constructed at the end of the Church.

SAN SILVESTRO IN CAPITE SAC (PALLOTTINES)

Piazza S. Silvestro, Rome 00187 Tel: 06-679-7775; Fax. 06-6979-9740; E-mail: Sansilvestro17@netscape.net

The Basilica of San Silvestro was designated as an English language church by Pope Leo XIII on 21 February 1885, and entrusted to the care of the Pallottines, a community founded by St Vincent Pallotti in 1839. There is also an active apostolate to the Italian community and to a large immigrant community from the Philippines and other countries.

THE CONGREGATION OF CHRISTIAN BROTHERS CFC

Via Marcantonio Colonna, 9, Rome 00192. Tel. 06-321.5669

The Christian Brothers came to Rome in 1900 on the invitation of the Pope's Vicar, Cardinal Jacobini. They established a day school and a night school for languages in Via Firenze. In 1907, they moved to a new residence and school that they had built at Via Marcantonio Colonna, in the developing area, not far from the Vatican. The night school for languages continued to flourish in Via Rasella up to 1923 when Benito Mussolini brought his family to Rome and installed them in an apartment in the same building that housed the Brothers' school. New accommodation for the night school was obtained in Via Olmata. Courses in English, French and German were provided right up to the time of World War II when they were obliged to terminate.

Istituto Marcantonio Colonna, in Via Marcantonio Colonna, prospered and earned a high reputation as a centre for education. Due to demographic changes in that area of Rome, the brothers closed the school in 1997 after nearly a century of service in education. Down through the years the brothers had also engaged in other works in Rome and in the Vatican. During and after World War II, some brothers worked with Mgr. Montini, later Pope Paul VI, dealing with correspondence regarding prisoners of war and some acted as Papal couriers to various capital cities in conflict areas. Since 1916, brothers have worked in the Prefecture of the Papal Household, as it is now called, in the office that administers invitations to Papal Functions and

Audiences. Brothers have also acted as Roman correspondents for various Catholic newspapers. Since 1985, brothers have been ministering in Boy's Town of Italy which is located near Rome.

In 1967, the Leadership of the Congregation transferred from Dublin to Rome, to Via della Maglianella and more recently to Via Marcantonio Colonna. International courses for the brothers were provided in Via della Maglianella. Blessed Edmund Rice, founder of the Christian Brothers and the Presentation Brothers, was beatified in 1996 and many thousands of friends of the brothers in Ireland, and in the many countries in which they have missions worldwide, came to Rome to join in the celebration.

St Patrick's Society SPS (Kiltegan Fathers)
Piazza de Villa Carpegna, 41, Rome 00165, Tel. 06-662.1797

St Columban's Society SSC (Columban Fathers)
Corso Trieste, 57, Rome 00198; Tel: 06-841-6603
The Missionary Society of St Columban, originally known as the Maynooth Mission to China, and popularly known today as the Columban Fathers, was founded in 1918 by two Irish diocesan priests, John Blowick, who was a priest of the Archdiocese of Tuam and a Professor at the National Seminary at Maynooth, and Edward J. Galvin, a priest of the Diocese of Cork who had worked in China for a number of years. Following approval by the Bishops of Ireland and the blessing of Pope Benedict XV, the young Society took the sixth-century Irish missionary, Saint Columban, as patron, and a seminary was established at Dalgan in the diocese of Galway. The seminary transferred to Dalgon Park, Navan, Co. Meath, in 1942. The Society was placed under what was then the Society for the Propagation of the Faith, now the Congregation for the Evangelization of Peoples, and granted pontifical status in 1925. The Society is a Society of Apostolic Life, a society of secular priests that is exclusively missionary. The Missionary Sisters of St Columban have worked closely with the priests in their missionary outreach.

Father Galvin returned to China in 1920 with the first group of sixteen Columban missionaries, who had responded to the call for volunteers. He became the first bishop of Hanyang when it was made a diocese in 1946. After many difficult years in China, during which some were called to give their lives for the faith, Bishop Galvin and all the remaining Columbans were expelled in 1952 following the rise of Communism. The Columbans, because of the political situation, were also compelled to leave Burma where they had been working since 1936. During this time Father Blowick, who had been elected Superior General at the first Chapter in 1919, served in various administrative and teaching posts until his death in 1972.

Members of the Society continue to work in the Republic of the Philippines, where they first went in 1929, and in Korea and Japan. In 1952 the Society began working in South America, Peru and Chile, and later in Brazil, where they have been joined by diocesan priests from many countries. At the same time an invitation to work with the peoples of the Fiji Islands was accepted. In more recent years members of the Society have undertaken missionary commitments in Taiwan, Pakistan, Belize and Jamaica. The College in Rome was established in 1932 as the residence of the Society's Procurator General and as a house for priests doing post-graduate studies.

Specific aims of Columban missionaries are preaching the Gospel to those who have not yet heard of Christ, accompanying the poor and marginalised in their struggle for justice and peace, the cancelling of the international debt which burdens poor countries, promoting the care of creation, fostering the lay missionary vocation in all the countries where they work, sending priests and sponsoring lay teachers to work in third-level educational institutes in China, and promoting indigenous missionary vocations in the countries where they first worked as missionaries.

REDEMPTORISTS CSsR
Via Merulana, 31, Rome 00185.
Tel. 06-494901; Fax. 06-49490-665
The Congregation of the Most Holy Redeemer, better known as the Redemptorists, was founded by St Alphonsus Liguori at Scala, near Salerno in Italy, in 1732. The aim was to preach the gospel to the poor, the neglected and the most spiritually deprived by means of missions, and spiritual exercises after the manner of St Paul. Redemptorists throughout the world now number 5800 members and are engaged in diverse apostolates among Christians and non-Christians. The first Irish Redemptorist foundation was made in Limerick in 1853 and Irish Redemptorists now minister not only in Ireland but also in Brazil, India, the Philippines and Nigeria.

The building on Via Merulana is the residence of the Superior General and his Council, and it also houses a college for post-graduate student priests as well as a Higher Institute of Moral Theology, the Accademia Alfonsiana, which was founded in 1949. The Donegal-born Patrick Murray, who was Superior General, lived here from 1909 until 1947. A well-known Irish professor was the late Sean O'Riordan. At present over eighty Redemptorists from thirty countries live and work in the College.

ROSMINIANS IC
Via di Porta Latina, 17, Rome 00179.
Tel. 06-7049-1777
The members of the Institute of Charity are usually referred to as Rosminians, after their founder, Antonio Rosmini (1797-1855). Rosmini, a renowned philosopher, was a friend of Cardinal Paul Cullen when the latter was a student at the Irish College. One of Rosmini's early companions, Luigi Gentili, studied for the priesthood at the Irish College and later preached retreats and missions in Ireland where he died of famine fever in 1848.

The Rosminian Missionary College at Porta Latina, opened in 1938 in a restored building dating to the beginning of the eighteenth century, has had many students from Ireland and four of the Rectors have been Irish. Nearby is the Basilica of St John of the Latin Gate and the Tempietto of St John in Oleo. Opposite the front of the house is the Garden of the Scipios which, in turn, opens on to the Via di S. Sebastiano and the Porta S. Sebastiano.

SOCIETY OF AFRICAN MISSION SMA
Via della Nocetta, 111, Rome 00164.
Tel. 06-661-6841; Fax. 06-6616-8490.

HOLY GHOST FATHERS CSSp
(Known also as the Congregation of the Holy Spirit, and increasingly internationally as the Spiritans)
Clivo di Cinna, 195, Rome 00136. Tel. 06-3540-461
The Congregation was founded in Paris on Pentecost Sunday 1703 by a seminarian, Claude Poullart des Places. It was dedicated to the Holy Spirit, under the protection of the Immaculate Heart of Mary, and committed to the training of poor seminarians for work in difficult situations in the French colonies. The young enthusiastic group flourished despite the early death of the Founder at the age of thirty. The Society suffered greatly as a result of persecution following the French Revolution in 1798 and it seemed the Society would cease to exist.
    In 1840 Jacob Libermann, the convert son of a Jewish Rabbi in Saverne, France, founded the Missionaries of the Holy Heart of Mary, dedicated to work in places where the slave trade was virulent, especially in the French colonies of Africa. Libermann brought the Rules of his Society to Rome for approval and was advised to join his Society with that of the Holy Spirit whose membership had dwindled. Both Societies had almost identical aims and both were dedicated to the Holy Heart of

Mary. Libermann agreed after much discussion and the union took place in 1848 to the great advantage of both Societies.

The Irish connection began in 1859 when the Society was seeking English-speaking members for some of its African missions. The Archbishop of Dublin welcomed them on condition that they would undertake some work in education for young Irish Catholics who had been deprived of schools following years of exclusion from education. Two French Spiritans arrived in 1859. Their founding of Blackrock College, known for many years as 'The French College', led to a deep commitment to education in Ireland and to a vast missionary outreach to Africa and later to other continents. Today the Irish Province of the Society has over 500 members working in 23 countries, in a total membership of over 3000 in 65 countries. The process of the beatification of Bishop Shanahan of Tipperary, one of the best known Irish members, was officially initiated at the cathedral in Onitsha in Nigeria in 1968.

In 1960 the official headquarters of the Society moved from Paris to Rome and is situated on Mount Mario, a hill overlooking the Vatican. The Assistant Superior General and the Secretary General are among the Irish members living there.

SECTION IV

A SELECTION OF PRAYERS AND
HYMNS FOR PILGRIMS

PRAYERS

Na Paidreacha Coitianta

Comhartha na Croise
In ainm an Athar agus an Mhic agus on Spioraid Naoimh. Amen.

An Phaidir
Ár n-Athair atá ar neamh,
go naofar d'ainm,
go dtaga do ríocht,
go ndéantar do thoil ar an talamh,
mar a dhéantar ar neamh.
Ár n-arán laethúil tabhair dúinn inniu,
agus maith dúinn ár bhfiacha,
mar a mhaithimídne dár bhféichiúna féin,
agus ná lig sinn i gcathú,
ach saor sinn ó olc. Amen

Fáilte an Aingil
'Sé do bheatha, a Mhuire, atá lán de ghrásta,
tá an Tiarna leat,
is beannaithe thú idir mhná,
agus is beannaithe toradh do bhruinne, Íosa.
A Naomh-Mhuire, a Mháthair De,
guidh orainn na peacaigh, anois agus ar uair ár mbáis.
Amen.

Glóir don Athair
Glóir don Athair, agus don Mhac, agus don Spiorad Naomh. Mar bhí ar dtús, mar atá anois, agus mar bhéas go bráth le saol no saol. Amen.

An Chré
Creidim in aon Dia amháin
an tAthair uilechumhachtach
a rinne neamh agus talamh
agus an uile ní sofheicthe agus dofheicthe.
Agus in aon Tiarna amháin,
Íosa Críost, Aon-Mhac Dé,
an té a rugadh ón Athair
sula raibh aon saol ann.

Dia ó Dhia, solas ó sholas, fíorDhia ó fhíorDhia;
an té a gineadh agus nach ndearnadh,
agus atá d'aon substaint leis an Athair;
is tríd a rinneach an uile ní.
Ar ár sonna an cine daonna,
agus ar son ár slánaithe,
thuirling sé ó neamh.
(Cromtar an ceann)
Ionchollaíodh le cumhacht an Spioraid Naoimh é
i mbroinn na Maighdine Muire
agus ghlac sé nádúr daonna.
Céasadh ar an gcrois é freisin ar ár son.
D'fhulaing sé páis faoi Phontius Píoláit
agus adhlacadh é.
D'aiséirigh and treas lá de réir na scioptúr.
Chuaigh sua ar neamh.
Tá ina shuí ar dheis an Athar.
Tiocfaidh sé an athuair faoi ghlóir
le breithiunas a thabhairt
ar bheo agus ar mhairbh
agus ní bheidh deireadh lena ríocht.
Creidim sa Spiorad Naomh,
Tiarna agus bronntóir na bheata,
an té a ghluaiseann ón Athair agus ón Mac.
Tugtar dó adhradh agus glóir
mar aon leis an Athair agus leis on Mac.
Is é a labhair trí na fáithe.
Creidim san aon Eaglais naofa, chaitliceach, aspalda.
Adhmhaím an t-aon bhaisteadh amháin
chun maithiúnas na bpeacaí.
Agus táim ag súil le haiséirí na marbh
agus le beatha an tsaoil atá le teacht Amen.

Hymns

1. Be Thou my Vision
Irish (6th century) tr. Mary Byrne, versified by Eleanor Hull

Be thou my vision, O Lord of my heart
be all else but naught to me,
save that thou art;
be thou my best thought in the day
and the night,
both waking and sleeping, thy presence my light.
By thou my wisdom, be thou my true word,
be thou ever with me, and I with thee, Lord;
be thou my great Father, and I thy true son,
be thou in me dwelling, and I with thee one.

Riches I need not, nor man's empty praise,
be thou mine inheritance now and all days;
be thou and thou only the first in my heart,
the King of high heaven, my treasure though art.

High King of heaven, thou heaven's bright sun.
O grant me its joys, after victory is won;
great heart of my own heart, whatever befall,
still be thou my vision, O ruler of all.

2. Come, Holy Spirit, Creator, Come

Come Holy Spirit, Creator, come,
Descend from heaven's throne.
Come take possession of our hearts,
And make them all your own.

You are the source of strength and might,
Great gift of God above.
You are the fount of truth and light,
The flame of hope and love.
O Spirit promised from of old,
we offer thanks to you.
You make us live, O Lord of life,
Your power makes all things new.

Then come great Spirit to your own,
Our hearts make pure and strong.
Direct our weary steps today,
And turn our wills from wrong.

Show us the Father and the Son,
O Spirit whom they send.
That in God's kingdom we may live
The life that knows no end.

All glory to the Father be,
With his eternal Son,
The same unto the Paraclete,
While endless ages run.

3. Come Adore this Wondrous Presence
St Thomas Aquinas (1227-74), translated by James Quinn, SJ
Copyright Geoffrey Chapman, a division of Casseell Publishers Ltd.

Come, adore this wondrous presence,
bow to Christ, the source of grace.
Here is kept the ancient promise
of God's earthly dwelling-place.
Sight is blind before God's glory,
faith alone may see his face.

Glory be to God the Father,
praise to his co-equal Son,
adoration to the Spirit,
bond of love, in Godhead one.
Blest be God by all creation
joyously while ages run.

4. Grant to Us, O Lord
Lucien Deiss (based on Ez 36:26 and Jer 31:31-34)
Copyright World Library

Grant to us, O Lord, a heart renewed;
recreate in us your own Spirit, Lord!

Behold the days are coming,
says the Lord our God

when I shall make a new covenant
with the house of Israel.

Deep within their being
I will implant my law;
I will write it on their hearts.

I will be their God,
and they shall be my people.

And for all their faults
I will grant forgiveness;
nevermore will I remember their sins.

5. I AM THE BREAD OF LIFE
Sister Suzanne Toolan, S.M. Copyright G.I.A. Publications

And I will raise you up, and I will raise you up,
and I will raise you up on the last day.

I am the Bread of Life. You who come to
me shall not hunger,
and who believe in me shall not thirst.
No one can come to me unless
the Father beckon

The bread that I will give is my flesh
for the life of the world,
and if you eat of this bread,
you shall live forever,
you shall live forever

Unless you eat of the flesh of the Son of Man
and drink of his blood, and drink of his blood,
you shall not have life within you.

I am the Resurrection, I am the life.
If you believe in me, even though you die,
you shall live forever.

Yes, Lord, I believe that you are the Christ,
the Son of God who have come into the world.

6. Keep in Mind
Lucien Deiss. Copyright World Library

Keep in mind that Jesus Christ has died for us
and is risen from the dead.
He is our saving Lord, he is joy for all ages.
If we die with the Lord,
we shall live with the Lord.

If we endure with the Lord,
we shall reign with the Lord.

In him all our sorrow, in him all our joy.

 In him hope of glory, in him all our love.

In him our redemption, in him all our grace.

In him our salvation, in him all our peace.

7. Christ be beside me
*Adapted from 'St Patrick's Breastplate' by James Quinn, S.J.
Copyright. Geoffrey Chapman, a division of Cassell Publishers Ltd.*

Christ be beside me, Christ be before me,
Christ be behind me, King of my heart.
Christ be within me, Christ be below me,
Christ be above me, never to part.

Christ on my right hand, Christ on my left hand,
Christ all around me, shield in the strife.
Christ in my sleeping, Christ in my sitting,
Christ in my rising, Light of my life.

Christ be in all hearts thinking about me.
Christ be on all tongues telling of me.
Christ be the vision in eyes that see me,
in ears that hear me, Christ ever be.

8. CÉAD MÍLE FÁILTE ROMHAT
Traidisiunta

Céad míle fáilte romhat, a Íosa, a Íosa,
céad míle fáilte romhat, a Íosa.
Céad míle fáilte romhat, a Shlánaitheoir,
céad míle míle fáilte romhat, Íosa, a Íosa.

Glóir and moladh duit, a Íosa, a Íosa,
glóir and moladh duit, a Íosa.
Glóir and moladh duit, a Shlánaitheoir,
glóir, moladh and buíochas duit, Íosa, a Íosa.

9. I'LL SING A HYMN TO MARY
F. Wyse-D. Murray. Copyright. Bishop Donal Murray

O Holy mother Mary
ask Christ your Son we pray
to grant us his forgiveness
and guide us on his way

I'll sing a hymn to Mary,
the mother of my God,
the virgin of all virgins,
of David's royal blood.

Rejoice, O holy Mary,
O Virgin full of grace,
the Lord is ever with you,
most blessed of our race.

10. LORD ACCEPT THE GIFTS WE OFFER
Sister M. Teresine

Lord accept the gifts we offer
at this Eucharistic feast,
bread and wine to be transformed now
through the action of thy priest,
take us too, Lord, and transform us,
be thy grace in us increased.

May our souls be pure and spotless

as the host of wheat so fine;
may all stain of sin be crushed out,
like the grape that forms the wine.
As we, too, become partakers,
in this sacrifice divine.

Take our gifts, almighty Father,
living God, eternal, true,
which we give through Christ our Saviour,
pleading here for us anew.
Grant salvation to all present,
and our faith and love renew.

11. MAKE ME A CHANNEL OF YOUR PEACE
Sebastian Temple. Copyright Franciscan Communications

Make me a channel of your peace.
Where there is hatred, let me bring your love.
Where there is injury, your pardon, Lord.
And where there's doubt, true faith in you.

Make me a channel of your peace.
Where there's despair in life, let me bring hope.
Where there is darkness only light,
and where there's sadness ever joy.

Oh, Master, grant that I may never seek
so much to be consoled as to console,
to be understood as to understand,
to be loved, as to love, with all my soul.

Make me a channel of your peace.
It is in pardoning that we are pardoned,
In giving to all that we receive,
and in dying that we are born to eternal life.

12. WHATSOEVER YOU DO
Copyright Willard F. Jabusch

Whatsoever you do
to the least of my brethren
that you do unto me.

When I was hungry you gave me to eat.
When I was thirsty you gave me to drink.
Now enter into the home of my Father.

When I was homeless you opened your door.
When I was naked you gave me your coat.
Now enter into the home of my Father.
When I was weary you helped me find rest.
When I was anxious you calmed all my fears.
Now enter into the home of my Father.

When in a prison you came to my cell.
When on a sick bed you cared for my needs.
Now enter into the home of my Father.

When I was aged you bothered to smile.
When I was restless you listened and cared.
Now enter into the home of my Father.

When I was laughed at you stood by my side.
When I was happy you shared in my joy.
Now enter into the home of my Father.

13. AG CRÍOST AN SÍOL
Traidisiúnta

Ag Críost an síol, ag Críost an fómhar,
in iothlainn Dé go dtugtar sinn.

Ag Críost an mhuir, ag Críost an t-iasc,
i líonta Dé go gcastar sinn.

Ó fhás go haois, is ó aois go bás
Do dhá láimh, a Críost, anall tharainn.

Ó bhás go críoch, ní críoch ach athfhás, i bParthas na Grást go
rabhaimid.

14. IOMANN

Dóchas linn Naomh Pádraig, aspal mór na hEireann,
Ainm oirdheare gléigeal, solas mór and tsaoil é.
D'fhill le soiscéal ghá dúinn ainneoin blianta i ngeibheann.
Grá mór Mhac na páirte d'fhuascail cách ón daorbhroid

Sléibhte, gleannta, maighe 's bailte mór na hEireann:
Ghlan sé iad go deo dúinn, míle glóir nár naomh dhil.
Iarraimid ort, a Phádraig, guí orainn na Gaela,
Dia linn lá 'gus oíche 's Pádraig aspall Eireann.

SECTION V

ROME JUBILEE 2000 CALENDAR

(Events planned by the Irish Communities in Rome are written in bold)

1999

DECEMBER

24 Christmas Vigil Mass in St Peter's
  Opening of the Holy Door

25 Christmas Morning Mass in Basilicas of St John Lateran and Mary Major
  Opening of the Holy Doors
  St Peter's Square (12 noon)
  Blessing 'Urbi et Orbi'

31 Basilica of St Peter
  Prayer Vigil to Usher in Year 2000

2000

JANUARY

1 Basilica of St Peter
  Solemnity of Mary Mother of God
  World Day of Prayer for Peace

2 Basilica of St Peter
  Children's Jubilee celebrations

6 Basilica of St Peter
  Solemnity of the Epiphany
  Episcopal Ordinations

9 Basilica of St Peter
  Feast of the Baptism of the Lord
  Baptism of Children

18 Basilica of St Paul Outside the Walls
  Week of Prayer for Christian Unity
  Opening of the Holy Door
  Ecumenical Service

25 Basilica of St Paul Outside the Walls
  Ecumenical Service
  Closing of Week of Prayer for Unity

28 Basilica of St Cecilia in Trastevere
  Liturgy in Chaldean and Malabar Rite

FEBRUARY

1 Church of San Clemente
  Feast of St Brigid

2 Basilica of St Peter

Feast of the Presentation of Our Lord
Jubilee Celebration of Consecrated Life

9   Basilica of St Mary Major
Liturgy in the Maronite Rite

11   Basilica of St Peter
Feast of Our Lady of Lourdes
Celebration of the Sacrament of the Sick.
Jubilee celebration for the Sick and all Health Workers.

18   Basilica of S. Maria sopra Minerva
Feast of the Blessed Fra Angelico
Jubilee celebration of Artists

22   Basilica of St Peter
Feast of the Chair of St Peter
Jubilee of the Roman Curia

25-27   *Symposium on Second Vatican Council*

MARCH

5   Basilica of St Peter
Beatifications/Canonisations

8   Penitential Procession from Basilica of St Sabina
to Circus Maximus
Ash Wednesday Liturgical Celebration

9   Basilica of St Paul Outside the Walls
Eucharistic Adoration

10   Basilica of St John Lateran
Way of the Cross and Penitential Service

11   Basilica of St Mary Major
Recitation of the Rosary
Celtic Ball - Charitable Dinner Dance

12   Basilica of St John Lateran
Nomination of Catechumens

16   Basilica of St Paul Outside the Walls
Eucharistic Adoration

17   Basilica of St John Lateran
Way of the Cross and Penitential Service
Feast of St Patrick

18   Basilica of St Mary Major
Recitation of the Rosary
The Irish College
History Commemoration - The First Millennium

20   Solemnity of St Joseph, Spouse of Mary
Jubilee of the Artisans

23	Basilica of St Paul Outside the Walls
	Eucharistic Adoration
25	Basilica of St Mary Major and Marian Sanctuaries
	throughout the world.
	Feast of The Annunciation
	Jubilee of the Dignity of Women
30	Basilica of St Paul Outside the Walls
	Eucharistic Adoration
31	Basilica of St John Lateran
	Way of the Cross and Penitential Service

APRIL

1	Basilica of St Mary Major
	Recitation of the Rosary
6	Basilica of St Paul Outside the Walls
	Eucharistic Adoration
7	Basilica of St John Lateran
	Way of the Cross and Penitential Service
8	Basilica of St Mary Major
	Recitation of the Rosary
10	*Jubilee celebration for Migrants and Refugees*
13	Basilica of St Paul Outside the Walls
	Eucharistic Adoration
14	Basilica of St John Lateran
	Way of the Cross and Penitential Service
15	Basilica of St Mary Major
	Recitation of the Rosary
16	St Peter's Square
	Palm Sunday
18	All Major Basilicas
	Penitential Services and Confession
20	Basilica of St Peter (a.m.)
	Mass of the Chrism
	Basilica of St John Lateran (p.m.)
	Mass of the Last Supper
21	Basilica of St Peter (p.m.)
	Celebration of the Passion of Our Lord
	Colosseum (night)
	Way of the Cross with the Holy Father
22	Basilica of St Peter
	Easter Vigil Liturgy
24	Basilica of St Peter

Mass of Easter Sunday
Blessing 'Urbi et Orbi'

30   Basilica of St Pancrazio
Mass for the newly baptised
Day of Pilgrimage for Irish in Rome

MAY

1   Feast of St Joseph the Worker
Jubilee celebration of Workers

6   Basilica of St Mary Major
Recitation of the Rosary

7   Colosseum
Ecumenical Commemoration of the 'New Martyrs'

13   Basilica of St Mary Major
Recitation of the Rosary

14   Basilica of St Peter
World Day of Prayer for Vocations
Ordinations to the Priesthood

18   St Peter's Square
Eightieth Birthday of the Holy Father
Jubilee of Members of the Clergy

20   Basilica of St Mary Major
Recitation of the Rosary

25   *Jubilee of the Scientists*

26   Basilica of St Mary of the Angels
Liturgy in the Alexandrian-Ethiopian Rite

27   Basilica of St Mary Major
Recitation of the Rosary

28   *Jubilee of the Diocese of Rome*

31   Basilica of St Peter
Vigil of the Ascension of Our Lord
First Vespers of the Solemnity

JUNE

1   Basilica of St Peter
Feast of the Ascension of Our Lord
Eucharist

4   World Day of Social Communications
Jubilee Celebrations of Journalists

9   **Feast of St Colmcille**
Ecumenical Service

10   St Peter's Square

	Solemn Vigil of Pentecost
11	St Peter's Square
	Feast of Pentecost
	World Day of Prayer for 'Inter-Religious' Dialogue
18	Basilica of St John Lateran
	Solemnity of the Blessed Trinity
	Opening of the International Eucharistic Congress
22	Basilica of St John Lateran
	Feast of the Body and Blood of Christ
	Eucharist Procession to St Mary Major
25	*Closure of Eucharistic Congress*
29	Basilica of St Peter
	Feast of Saints, Peter and Paul
	Eucharist

JULY

9	Jubilee Celebration in Prisons
16	***Irish Picnic Day in Rome***

AUGUST

5	Basilica of St Mary Major
	Vigil of the Transfiguration of Christ
	Prayer Vigil
6	Basilica of St Paul Outside the Walls
	Feast of the Transfiguration of Christ
	Second Vespers of the Feast
14	Basilica of St Mary Major
	Vigil of the Feast of the Assumption
	Coptic Liturgy
15	Feast of the Assumption of Our Lady
	Opening of 15th World Youth Celebration
19-20	*Vigil of Prayer*
	Conclusion of World Youth Celebration
	Youth Jubilee Celebration

SEPTEMBER

3	Basilica of St Peter
	Beatifications – Canonisations
8	Feast of the Nativity of the Virgin Mary
	Celebration of the Birth of the Mother of Our Saviour Jesus Christ
10	Basilica of St Peter
	Jubilee Celebration of University Teachers

12	*Thanksgiving for the gifts of Creation and Jubilee Celebration of the Agricultural World*
19	Basilica of St Peter *Jubilee Celebration of the Military and Police with Mass*
21	Basilica of St Mary in Trastevere Feast of the Presentation of the Blessed Virgin Mary *Liturgy in Syrian and Malanker Rite*
23	**Feast of St Columbanus** ***Pilgrimage to Bobbio***
24	*Opening of the World Congress of the Apostolate of the Laity*
26	Basilica of St Peter *Closure of the Congress of the Laity with Mass*

DECEMBER

Advent Services

2	Basilica of St Peter Vigil of the First Sunday of Advent *First Vespers of Sunday*
3	Basilica of St Paul Outside the Walls *Mass*
8	Basilica of St Mary Major Feast of the Immaculate Conception of the Blessed Virgin Mary *Mass*
10	Basilica of St Mary Major *Mass*
16	Basilica of St Mary Major *Celebration in Mozarabic Rite*
17	Basilica of St Paul Outside the Walls *Jubilee Celebration of Show Business with Mass*
24	Feast of the Nativity of Our Lord Basilica of St Peter *Midnight Mass*
25	Basilica of St Peter Feast of the Nativity *Mass of the Day* *Blessing 'Urbi et Orbi'*
31	Basilica of St Peter *Vigil of Prayer for the End of 2000*

1 Basilica of St Peter
  Feast of Mary the Mother of God
  World Day of Prayer for Peace
  Mass

5 Vigil of the Feast of the Epiphany
  Closure of the Holy Doors in Basilicas and Churches, except in
  the Basilica of St Peter, Rome

6 Basilica of St Peter
  Feast of the Epiphany of Our Lord
  Closure of the Holy Door

INDEX